# Oxford AQA GCSE History

# Britain: Health and the People c1000-Present Day

# Revision Guide

 RECAP   APPLY   REVIEW   SUCCEED

UPDATED

**Changes to the AQA GCSE History specification 8145 (Version 1.3) and support for these changes**

AQA released Version 1.3 of their AQA GCSE History specification in September 2019. The changes are to the command words and stems to a number of the AQA GCSE History questions to make the demands of the questions clearer for all students. Please refer to the AQA website for more information.

To support you with these changes, we have reviewed the content of this book and made the necessary small amends.

AUTHOR & SERIES EDITOR
**Aaron Wilkes**

**OXFORD**

Great Clarendon Street, Oxford, OX2 6DP, United Kingdom

Oxford University Press is a department of the University of Oxford.

It furthers the University's objective of excellence in research, scholarship, and education by publishing worldwide. Oxford is a registered trade mark of Oxford University Press in the UK and in certain other countries.

British Library Cataloguing in Publication Data

Data available

978-0-19-842295-2

Digital edition 978-0-19-842296-9

11

Paper used in the production of this book is a natural, recyclable product made from wood grown in sustainable forests.

The manufacturing process conforms to the environmental regulations of the country of origin.

Printed in China by Shanghai Offset Printing Products Ltd

**Acknowledgements**

The publisher would like to thank Jon Cloake for his work on the Student Book on which this Revision Guide is based and Lindsay Bruce for reviewing this Revision Guide.

The publishers would like to thank the following for permissions to use their photographs:

**Cover:** Print Collector/Getty Images

**Photos: p13:** A Ward in the Hotel-Dieu, Paris, from 'Science and Literature in the Middle Ages and Renaissance', written and engraved by Paul Lacroix (engraving) (b/w photo), French School, (16th century) (after) /Bibliotheque des Arts Decoratifs, Paris, France / Bridgeman Images; **p16:** Ms Sup Turc 693 fol.76v Excision of a ranula from under the tongue, 1466 (vellum), Charaf-ed-Din (1404-68) / Bibliotheque Nationale, Paris, France / Archives Charmet / Bridgeman Images; **p17:** Science Photo Library; **p23:** Science History Images/ Alamy Stock Photo; **p24 (L):** ResearchedPortrait Essentials/Alamy Stock Photo; **p24 (R):** Science History Images/Alamy Stock Photo; **p29:** National Portrait Gallery; **p30:** Wellcome Library, London; **p34:** age fotostock/Alamy Stock Photo; **p39:** Hulton Archive/Getty; **p43:** Public Health Act, 1848: The Home Secretary, Lord Morpeth, casting pearls (the provisons of the Act) before swine (the City of London Aldermen). Cartoon from Punch, London, 1848./Universal History Archive/UIG/Bridgeman Images; **p45:** Popperfoto/ Getty; **p46:** Bettman/Corbis; **p53:** The National Archives/Getty; **p55:** The National Archives; **p58:** Amaret Tanner/Alamy Stock Photo

**Artworks:** Aptara

Although we have made every effort to trace and contact all copyright holders before publication this has not been possible in all cases. If notified, the publisher will rectify any errors or omissions at the earliest opportunity.

# Contents

Introduction to this Revision Guide . . . . . . . . . . . . . . . . . . . . . . . . . . . . . . . . .5

Top revision tips . . . . . . . . . . . . . . . . . . . . . . . . . . . . . . . . . . . . . . . . . . . . . . .6

Master your exam skills . . . . . . . . . . . . . . . . . . . . . . . . . . . . . . . . . . . . . . . . . 7

How to master the source question. . . . . . . . . . . . . . . . . . . . . . . . . . . . . . . . . 7

How to master the significance question. . . . . . . . . . . . . . . . . . . . . . . . . . . . . 8

How to master the similarity/difference question. . . . . . . . . . . . . . . . . . . . . . 8

How to master the main factors question . . . . . . . . . . . . . . . . . . . . . . . . . . . . 9

AQA GCSE mark schemes . . . . . . . . . . . . . . . . . . . . . . . . . . . . . . . . . . . . . . .10

Health and the People c1000–Present Day Timeline . . . . . . . . . . . . . . . . . . . . .11

**RECAP**    **APPLY**    **REVIEW**

## Part one:
### Medicine stands still

**1   Medieval medicine**     12

   Treating the sick in Medieval England . . . . . . . . . . . . . . . . . . . . . . . . . . . .12

**2   Medical progress**     14

   The influence of Islam on Medieval medicine . . . . . . . . . . . . . . . . . . . . . . .14

   Limitations of Medieval surgery. . . . . . . . . . . . . . . . . . . . . . . . . . . . . . . . .16

**3   Public health in the Middle Ages**     18

   Public health in Medieval towns, Conditions in monasteries and abbeys . . . . .18

   The Black Death in Britain. . . . . . . . . . . . . . . . . . . . . . . . . . . . . . . . . . . . 20

## Part two:
### The beginnings of change

**4   The impact of the Renaissance on Britain**     22

   The work of Vesalius. . . . . . . . . . . . . . . . . . . . . . . . . . . . . . . . . . . . . . . . . 22

   Renaissance surgery and physiology, Paré's contribution to medical
   progress in England, Harvey's contribution to medical progress . . . . . . . . . . .24

**5   Dealing with disease**     26

   Traditional and new treatments, The Great Plague. . . . . . . . . . . . . . . . . . . 26

   Hospitals in the eighteenth century, John Hunter. . . . . . . . . . . . . . . . . . . . 28

**6   Prevention of disease**     30

   Edward Jenner and the prevention of smallpox, Inoculation,
   Jenner's discovery of vaccination . . . . . . . . . . . . . . . . . . . . . . . . . . . . . . . 30

   Reasons for opposition to Jenner and vaccination . . . . . . . . . . . . . . . . . . . 31

# Contents

## Part three:
### A revolution in medicine

|  |  |  | RECAP | APPLY | REVIEW |
|---|---|---|:---:|:---:|:---:|

**7** Advances in medical science in nineteenth-century Britain — 32

    The problem of pain, The reasons for the opposition to anaesthetics ...... 32 ○ ○ ○

    Louis Pasteur's Germ Theory, Germ Theory in Britain:
        Joseph Lister, Reasons for opposition to antiseptic surgery......... 34 ○ ○ ○

    Louis Pasteur and the Germ Theory debate, Aseptic surgery.............. 36 ○ ○ ○

**8** Further impact of Germ Theory in Britain — 38

    Robert Koch ...................... 38 ○ ○ ○

**9** Improvements in public health — 40

    Cholera and public health..................... 40 ○ ○ ○

    Governments and public health in the nineteenth century ............... 42 ○ ○ ○

    The 1875 Public Health Act....................... 43 ○ ○ ○

## Part four:
### Modern medicine

**10** Modern treatment of disease — 44

    The development of penicillin .......................... 46 ○ ○ ○

    The development of the pharmaceutical industry........................ 47 ○ ○ ○

    Antibiotic resistance, Alternative treatments and positive health ........ 49 ○ ○ ○

**11** The impact of war and technology on surgery — 50

    Wartime developments: plastic surgery, blood transfusions and X-rays ... 50 ○ ○ ○

    Modern surgical methods, Transplant surgery......................... 52 ○ ○ ○

**12** Modern public health — 54

    The reports of Booth and Rowntree, The Boer War, The Liberal Reforms.... 54 ○ ○ ○

    The welfare state, Impact of two world wars on public health,
    Development of the NHS................................ 56 ○ ○ ○

    **Exam practice:** GCSE sample answers................................ 58 ○ ○ ○

    Activity answers guidance........................... 63

    Glossary ....................... 68

# Introduction

The *Oxford AQA GCSE History* textbook series has been developed by an expert team led by Jon Cloake and Aaron Wilkes. This matching revision guide offers you step-by-step strategies to master your AQA Thematic Study: Health and the People exam skills, and the structured revision approach of **Recap, Apply and Review** to prepare you for exam success.

Use the **Progress checklists** on pages 3–4 to keep track of your revision, and use the traffic light ○ ○ ○ feature on each page to monitor your confidence level on each topic. Other exam practice and revision features include **Top revision tips** on page 6, and the '**How to...**' guides for each exam question type on pages 7–9.

 **RECAP**    Each chapter recaps key events and developments through easy-to-digest chunks and visual diagrams. **Key terms** appear in bold and red font; they are defined in the glossary. 📖 indicates the relevant Oxford AQA History Student Book pages so you could easily re-read the textbook for further revision.

**SUMMARY** highlights the most important facts at the end of each chapter.

**TIMELINE** ⏱ provides a short list of dates to help you remember key events.

 **APPLY**    Each revision activity is designed to help drill your understanding of facts, and then progress towards applying your knowledge to exam questions.

These targeted revision activities are written specifically for this guide, which will help you apply your knowledge towards the four exam questions in your AQA Health and the People exam paper:

**SOURCE ANALYSIS**    **EXPLAIN THE SIGNIFICANCE**    **SIMILARITY/DIFFERENCE**    **FACTORS**

 **Examiner Tip** highlights key parts of an exam question, and gives you hints on how to avoid common mistakes in exams.

 **Revision Skills** provides different revision techniques. Research shows that using a variety of revision styles can help cement your revision.

 **Review** gives you helpful reminders about how to check your answers and how to revise further.

 **REVIEW**    Throughout each chapter, you can review and reflect on the work you have done, and find advice on how to further refresh your knowledge.

You can tick off the Review column from the Progress checklists as you work through this revision guide. **Activity answers guidance** and the **Exam practice** sections with full sample student answers also help you to review your own work.

# Top revision tips

## Getting your revision right

It is perfectly natural to feel anxious when exam time approaches. The best way to keep on top of the stress is to be organised!

### 3 months to go

**Plan:** create a realistic revision timetable, and stick to it!

**Track your progress:** use the Progress Checklists (pages 3–4) to help you track your revision. It will help you stick to your revision plan.

**Be realistic:** revise in regular, small chunks, of around 30 minutes. Reward yourself with 10 minute breaks – you will be amazed how much more you'll remember.

**Positive thinking:** motivate yourself by turning your negative thoughts to positive ones. Instead of asking *'why can't I remember this topic at all?'* ask yourself *'what different techniques can I try to improve my memory?'*

**Organise:** make sure you have everything you need – your revision books, coloured pens, index cards, sticky notes, paper, etc. Find a quiet place where you are comfortable. Divide your notes into sections that are easy to use.

**Timeline:** create a timeline with colour-coded sticky notes, to make sure you remember important dates relating to the three parts of the Germany period study (use the Timeline on page 11 as a starting point).

**Practise:** ask your teachers for practice questions or past papers.

### Revision techniques

Using a variety of revision techniques can help you remember information, so try out different methods:

- Make **flashcards**, using both sides of the card to test yourself on key figures, dates, and definitions
- **Colour-code** your notebooks
- **Reread** your textbook or copy out your notes
- Create **mind-maps** for complicated topics
- Draw **pictures** and symbols that spring to mind
- Group study
- Find a **buddy** or group to revise with and test you
- Listen to revision **podcasts** or watch revision **clips**
- Work through the **revision activities** in this guide.

## Revision tips to help you pass your Health and the People exam ☑

### 1 month to go

**Big picture:** make sure you are familiar with examples – from the different periods you have studied – of the factors relating to this Thematic Study: war; superstition and religion; chance; government; communication; science and technology; the role of the individual in encouraging or inhibiting change.

**Identify your weaknesses:** which topics or question types are easier and which are more challenging for you? Schedule more time to revise the challenging topics or question types.

**Make it stick:** find memorable ways to remember chronology, using fun rhymes, or doodles, for example.

**Take a break:** do something completely different during breaks – listen to music, take a short walk, make a cup of tea, for example.

**Check your answers:** answer the exam questions in this guide, then check the Activity answers guidance at the end of the guide to practise applying your knowledge to exam questions.

**Understand your mark scheme:** review the Mark scheme (page 10) for each exam question, and make sure you understand how you will be marked.

**Master your exam skills:** study and remember the How to master your exam skills steps (pages 7–9) for each AQA question type – it will help you plan your answers quickly!

**Time yourself:** practise making plans and answering exam questions within the recommended time limits.

**Take mock exams seriously:** you can learn from them how to manage your time better under exam conditions.

**Rest well:** make sure your phone and laptop are put away at least an hour before bed. This will help you rest better.

### On the big day

**Sleep early:** Don't work through the night, get a good night's sleep.

**Be prepared:** Make sure you know where and when the exam is, and leave plenty of time to get there.

**Check:** make sure you have all your equipment in advance, including spare pens!

**Drink and eat healthily:** avoid too much caffeine or junk food. Water is best – if you are 5% dehydrated, then your concentration drops 20%.

**Stay focused:** don't listen to people who might try to wind you up about what might come up in the exam – they don't know any more than you.

**Good luck!**

# Master your exam skills

## Get to grips with your Paper 2: Health and the People Thematic Study

The Paper 2 exam lasts 2 hours, and you must answer 8 questions covering 2 topics. The first 4 questions (worth 44 marks) will cover the Thematic Study; the last 4 questions (40 marks) will cover your British Depth Study topic. Here, you will find details about what to expect from the first 4 questions which relate to the Health and the People Thematic Study, and advice on how to master your exam skills.

You should spend about 50 minutes in total on the Health and the People questions — see pages 58–62 for how long to spend on each question. The 4 questions will always follow this pattern:

▼ **SOURCE A**

01   Study **Source A**. How useful is **Source A** to a historian studying …? Explain your answer using **Source A** and your contextual knowledge.

[8 marks]

02   Explain the significance of … [8 marks]

03   Explain **two ways** in which… were similar/different. [8 marks]

04   Has … been the main factor in …? Explain your answer with reference to … and other factors. [16 marks] [SPaG 4 marks]

**REVISION SKILLS**

Read the British Depth Study Revision Guide for help on the last 4 questions of Paper 2.

**EXAMINER TIP**

Remember that this question is similar to the source question in Paper 1, but this focuses on just *one* source.

**EXAMINER TIP**

This question requires you to think about the significance of something. You have to consider the contemporary, short- and long-term impact of an event or development.

## REVIEW

If you find FACTORS challenging, look out for the FACTORS activities throughout this guide to help you revise and drill your understanding of the FACTORS questions. Look out for the REVISION SKILLS tips too, to inspire you to find the revision strategies that work for you!

**EXAMINER TIP**

This question is worth a lot of marks and requires a longer answer. Make sure you leave plenty of time to complete it at the end of the exam. Don't forget that you get up to 4 marks for spelling, punctuation and grammar (SPaG) on this question too.

## How to master the source question

This question targets your understanding of how useful the source is to a historian. Usually, the source will be an image (a cartoon or drawing, for example), but in some years a textual source may be used. Here are the steps to consider when answering the source question.

### Question 1

- **Content:** Look at the source carefully. What point is the artist or writer making about the subject? Circle or underline any key points or arguments that are made.

- **Provenance:** Consider the time in which the source was created. What topic or event does the source relate to? Use the provenance (caption) of the source to think about where the source was created, the circumstances of the creator, how much information they had, and their purpose and audience.

- **Context:** Now think back over your own knowledge. Write about whether the content and caption fit with what you know. Does it give a fair reflection of the person, event or issue it describes?

- **Comment:** You need to make a judgement about how useful the source is. A good way to work towards an answer is to think about what is 'inside' the source (that may be the image or text) and what is 'outside' the source (the provenance). These two pieces of information affect the usefulness of a source for a historian studying a particular topic.
- ⏱ Spend about 10 minutes answering this 8-mark question.

# How to master the 'significance' question

Judging the significance of a person or event is about looking at the impact that the person/event had *at the time*, how it affected people *in the long term*, and whether it is still relevant *today*. Here are the steps to consider for answering the 'significance' question.

### Question 2

- **Plan:** Consider the immediate importance or impact (short term) of a person/event and their importance later on (long term). Look at the diagram carefully to help you plan:

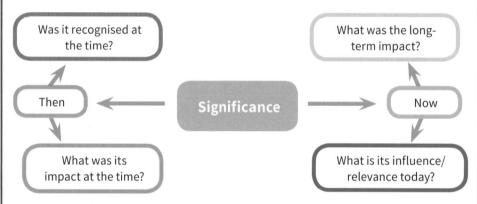

- **Explain the significance:** You need to say what *impact* the person/event made, and whether it had an impact at the time and/or now. In what ways did it have an impact on the wider historical period? Did it affect people's lives? Did it have an impact on politics or the government? Did it lead to change? What happened as a result of it?
- ⏱ Spend about 10 minutes answering this 8-mark question.

# How to master the 'similarity/difference' question

Here are the steps to consider for answering the 'similarity/difference' question. This question asks you to consider the similarities or differences between two events or developments.

### Question 3

- **Plan**: Make a list or a mindmap to help you analyse the similarities or differences between the two events/developments. What historical facts do you know about the similarities or differences for each of the event/development?
- **Write**: When you have chosen two similarities or differences you want to write about, organise them into two paragraphs, one for each. Consider these points for each paragraph:
  - **Causes:** think about the ways in which the two events have similar or different causes.

- **Development:** consider what you know about what happened in both events. Look for points of similarity or difference that you can identify and explain.

- **Consequences:** think about the results of the events – again identify and explain similarities or differences.

- ⏱ Spend about 10 minutes answering this 8-mark question.

# How to master the 'main factors' question

The last question on Health and the People in Paper 2 is a question on 'main factors'. It carries the highest mark, along with 4 marks for spelling, punctuation and grammar. The question gives you the opportunity to 'show off' your knowledge of the whole Health and the People Thematic Study and select information that shows the influence of factors in history, such as religion, war, chance, government, communication, science and technology, and the role of the individual.

## Question 4

- **Read the question carefully:** The question will name one factor. Circle the named factor. What topic is the question asking you to consider? The topic is located at the end of the first sentence. Underline the topic to help you focus your answer.

- **Plan your essay:** You could plan your essay by listing the named factor and other factors that caused the event/issue stated in the question:

| Named factor 1 | Another factor 2 | Another factor 3 |
|---|---|---|
| | | |

Write in anything you could use as evidence for the different factors, but make sure that your answer is relevant to the topic of the Thematic Study that has been asked in the question (the one you underlined).

- **Write your essay:** Aim for about four paragraphs. First, write about the influence of the named factor in relation to the topic asked in the question. Write a paragraph each about two more factors in addition to the one named in the question. Lastly, you will have to come to a judgement (a clear conclusion) about whether you agree that the named factor was the main factor. Try to weigh up the named factor against the other ones you wrote about, and say which was more important.

- **Check your SPaG:** Don't forget that you get up to 4 marks for your SPaG in this answer. It's a good idea to leave time to check your SPaG.

- ⏱ This question is worth 16 marks plus 4 SPaG marks. Spend around 20 minutes on it, but this needs to include time to plan and to check your SPaG.

**EXAMINER TIP**

Remember that you only have about 2–3 minutes to plan and 15–17 minutes to write your paragraphs. For each factor, choose two historical facts from the history of Health and the People you are most confident about, and highlight these.

**EXAMINER TIP**

To back up your conclusion, you should explain *why* you came to that judgement, with supporting evidence. Answers that demonstrate a broad knowledge of examples from across the whole Thematic Study are more likely to gain higher marks.

**EXAMINER TIP**

Don't forget you will have to answer 4 more questions, relating to your British Depth Study topic, in Paper 2. Ensure you leave enough time to complete both sections of Paper 2! You are advised to spend 50 minutes on your British Depth Study.

**REVIEW**

You can find sample student answers to each Health and the People question type in the Exam practice pages at the end of this Revision Guide.

# AQA GCSE History mark schemes

Below are simplified versions of the AQA mark schemes, to help you understand the marking criteria for your **Paper 2 Britain: Health and the People Thematic Study** exam.

| Level | Question 1  Source question |
|---|---|
| 4 | • Complex evaluation of the source<br>• Argument is shown throughout the answer about how useful the source is, supported by evidence from provenance *and* content, and relevant facts    [7–8 marks] |
| 3 | • Developed evaluation of the source<br>• Argument is stated about how useful the source is, supported by evidence from source content and/or provenance    [5–6 marks] |
| 2 | • Simple evaluation of source<br>• Answer is shown about how useful the source is, based on content and/or provenance    [3–4 marks] |
| 1 | • Basic analysis on the source<br>• Basic description of the source is shown    [1–2 marks] |

| Level | Question 2  Significance question |
|---|---|
| 4 | • Complex explanation of aspects of significance<br>• A range of accurate, detailed and relevant facts are shown    [7–8 marks] |
| 3 | • Developed explanation of aspects of significance<br>• A range of accurate, relevant facts are shown    [5–6 marks] |
| 2 | • Simple explanation of one aspect of significance<br>• Specific relevant facts are shown    [3–4 marks] |
| 1 | • Basic explanation of aspect(s) of significance<br>• Some basic related facts are shown    [1–2 marks] |

| Level | Question 3  Similarity/difference question |
|---|---|
| 4 | • Complex explanation of similarities or differences<br>• A range of accurate, detailed and relevant facts are shown    [7–8 marks] |
| 3 | • Developed explanation of similarities or differences<br>• A range of accurate, relevant facts are shown    [5–6 marks] |
| 2 | • Simple explanation of one similarity or difference<br>• Specific relevant facts are shown    [3–4 marks] |
| 1 | • Basic explanation of similarity or difference<br>• Some basic related facts are shown    [1–2 marks] |

| Level | Question 4  Main factors question |
|---|---|
| 4 | • Complex explanation of named factor *and* other factor(s)<br>• Argument is shown throughout the structured answer, supported by a range of accurate, detailed and relevant facts    [13–16 marks] |
| 3 | • Developed explanation of the named factor *and* other factor(s)<br>• Argument is shown throughout the structured answer, supported by a range of accurate and relevant facts    [9–12 marks] |
| 2 | • Simple explanation of the stated factor or other factor(s)<br>• Argument is shown, supported by relevant facts    [5–8 marks] |
| 1 | • Basic explanation of one or more factors<br>• Some basic facts are shown    [1–4 marks] |

You also achieve up to 4 marks for spelling, punctuation and grammar (SPaG) on the main factors question:

| Level | Question 4 Main factors question SPaG marks |
|---|---|
| Excellent | • SPaG is accurate throughout the answer<br>• Meaning is very clear<br>• A *wide* range of key historical terms are used accurately    [4 marks] |
| Good | • SPaG shown with considerable accuracy<br>• Meaning is generally clear<br>• A range of key historical terms are used    [2–3 marks] |
| Satisfactory | • SPaG shown with some accuracy<br>• SPaG allows historical understanding to be shown<br>• Basic historical terms are used    [1 marks] |

# Britain: Health and the People c1000–Present Day Timeline

The symbols represent different types of event as follows:

 Red: surgery  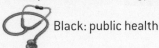  Black: public health   Yellow: disease

**c1230**  *Compendium Medicine* is written by Gilbert Eagle – a comprehensive English medical textbook blending European and Arab knowledge of medicine

**1348**  Black Death arrives in England

**1628**  William Harvey proves the circulation of the blood

**1724**  Guy's Hospital is founded in London

**1798**  Edward Jenner develops cowpox as a protection against smallpox

**1847**  James Simpson uses chloroform as an anaesthetic

**1848**  First Public Health Act is introduced

**1858**  Joseph Bazalgette begins building a network of sewers under London's streets

**1867**  Joseph Lister publishes a description of carbolic antiseptic in surgery

**1882**  Robert Koch's work on the identification of tuberculosis is publicised in Britain

**1906**  First of the Liberal social reforms – including free school meals for the poorest children, free medical checks and free treatment – is introduced

**1928**  Alexander Fleming discovers that penicillin kills bacteria

**1948**  NHS comes into operation

**1953**  Francis Crick and James Watson publish their research on the structure of DNA

**1963** First liver transplant is carried out in America

**2003**  Human Genome Project is declared complete with the final sequencing of the entire human genome; this is a huge breakthrough in understanding how genes help determine who a person is

## CHAPTER 1

# Medieval medicine

## Treating the sick in Medieval England

There was a variety of different people you went to if you were ill in Medieval Britain – and an even greater variety of treatments:

- **Barber surgeons in towns** – did **bloodletting**, minor surgery; based on experience.
- **Wise men or women in the village** – gave first aid, herbal remedies, supernatural cures with charms and spells based on tradition; based on word-of-mouth and trial and error.
- **Travelling healers in markets and fairs** – extracted teeth, sold potions, mended dislocations or fractures.
- **Herbalists in monasteries** – used herbal treatments, bloodletting, prayer and rest in the infirmary; based on the ancient knowledge of books like Pliny's *Natural History*, word-of-mouth, and experience.
- **Trained doctors in large towns** – treated using Hippocratic and Galenic methods from British textbooks such as Gilbert Eagle's *Compendium Medicine* (c1230) and Islamic texts such as Avicenna's *Canon of Medicine*.
  - Very **few** doctors in Medieval England.
  - Charged **fees** for services.
  - Studied for at least **seven years** at universities controlled by the Christian Church – the main religion in Western Europe.

| Medieval treatments showed a belief in both the **natural** and **supernatural** causes of disease | |
|---|---|
| Natural | Supernatural |
| Christian Church approved of the knowledge of the ancient Greeks and Romans; Galen, although he lived in Roman times, believed in one God; this fitted with Christian ideas | Many diseases that Hippocratic and Galenic medicine could not cure; for these diseases supernatural ideas influenced doctors' treatments |
| Doctors used: <br> • clinical observation – checking pulse and urine <br> • four **humours** | Doctors checked: <br> • position of the stars <br> • recommended charms and prayers |

Medieval doctors based their natural cures on the Ancient Greek theory of illness, which involved the equal balance of the body's four 'humours' – blood, phlegm, black bile and yellow bile. They believed that a person became ill when these were out of balance, and the doctor's job was to restore this balance.

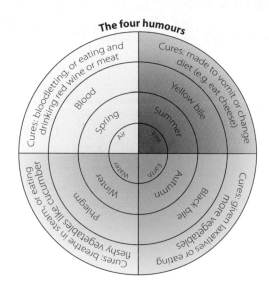

The four humours

## How did Christianity affect Medieval medicine?

 The Christian Church believed in following the example of Jesus who healed the sick; therefore Christians believed it was good to look after the sick

 God sent illness as a punishment (e.g. mental illness) or a test of faith, so curing an illness would challenge God's will

Monks preserved and copied by hand ancient medical texts

Prayers were the most important treatment rather than drugs

 Christians believed in caring for the sick and started many hospitals; over 700 were set up in England between 1000 and 1500

 The Church believed in miraculous healing and the sick were encouraged to visit shrines (a **pilgrimage**) with the relics of a holy person, and pray to saints to cure their illness

Hospitals were funded by the Church or a wealthy patron; for example St Leonard's hospital was paid for by the Norman King Stephen

Hospitals concentrated on caring for the sick and not curing; many had a priest rather than a doctor

The Church arrested the thirteenth-century English monk, Roger Bacon, for suggesting doctors should do original research and not trust old books

The Church approved the medical ideas of the ancient Greeks and Romans; their ideas were taught in the universities

## APPLY

### SOURCE ANALYSIS

◄ **SOURCE A**

*An illustration from c1500 of the Hotel Dieu in Paris, a late Medieval hospital; the French king's doctors worked there*

**a** Identify two Christian details in the picture.

**b**

EXAM QUESTION Study **Source A**. How useful is **Source A** for understanding Medieval ideas about illness?

### EXAMINER TIP

Try to link something you can see in the picture with the provenance and your own knowledge.

### FACTORS

Draw a table to show whether Christianity in the Middle Ages helped or hindered medical progress and treatments.

| Christianity helped medical progress and treatments | Christianity hindered medical progress and treatments |
|---|---|
| | |
| | |

### EXAMINER TIP

You will need to explain the influence of different factors on medical developments in your exam. This table will help you organise and remember how religion had an impact on medicine.

## CHAPTER 2

# Medical progress

📖 **RECAP**

## The influence of Islam on Medieval medicine

While Western Europe entered a period known as the Early Middle Ages, the followers of Islam established an enormous and unified Islamic Empire. Islamic doctors made great contributions to medical knowledge.

**Timeline:** ⏱️

**▼ 786–809**

- ◼ Reign of Caliph Harun al-Rashid: Baghdad became a centre for the translation of Greek manuscripts into the language of Islam (Arabic)

**▼ 805**

- ◼ Al-Rashid set up a major new hospital in Baghdad with a medical school and library

**▼ 813-33**

- ◼ Reign of Caliph al-Mamum:
  - developed al-Rashid's library into 'The House of Wisdom' – the world's largest library and a study centre for scholars
  - preserved hundreds of ancient Greek medical books by Hippocrates and Galen, which were lost to Western Europe during the Early Middle Ages

## Islamic ideas about medicine

- The Islamic religion encouraged medical learning and discoveries: the Prophet Muhammad said, 'For every disease, Allah has given a cure.' So doctors were inspired to find them.
- Muslim scientists were encouraged to discover cures and new drugs, such as senna and naphtha.
- In the Islamic Empire people with mental illnesses were treated with compassion.
- Islamic medicine valued Hippocratic and Galenic medicine, and it preserved and learned from the books of the ancient world.
- Muslim hospitals called **bimaristans** were meant for treating patients, not simply caring for them as was the case in the Christian world.

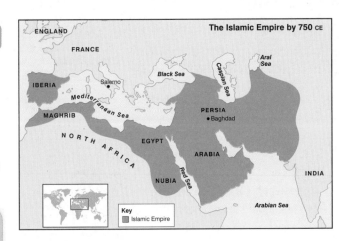

## How did Islamic medical knowledge spread?

Islamic medical discoveries, and the old medical knowledge of the ancient Greeks, arrived in Italy around 1065 through the Latin translations of a merchant, Constantine the African

The universities in Padua and Bologna in Italy soon became the best places to study medicine in Medieval Europe

These medical ideas reached England through trade, as merchants brought new equipment, drugs and books

# Important Islamic doctors

**Rhazes (c865–c925):**

- distinguished measles from smallpox for the first time
- wrote over 150 books
- followed Galen, but was critical; one of his books was called *Doubts about Galen*.

**Avicenna (980–1037):**

- wrote a great encyclopaedia of ancient Greek and Islamic medicine known as *Canon of Medicine*
- this listed the medical properties of 760 different drugs (such as camphor and laudanum), and discussed anorexia and obesity

- it became the standard European medical textbook used to teach doctors in the West until the seventeenth century.

**Ibn al-Nafis:**

- in the thirteenth century, he concluded that Galen was wrong about how the heart worked, claiming that blood circulated via the lungs
- but Islam did not allow human dissection and his books were not read in the West
- Europeans continued to accept Galen's mistake until the seventeenth century.

 **APPLY**

**REVISION SKILLS**

Making **revision cards** is a good way of revising and creating a useful revision aid for later use. Write a heading/topic on the front of each card, and on the back, jot down three or four things related to the topic. Try to include a factual detail with each point.

**EXPLAIN THE SIGNIFICANCE**

**a** Identify two ways in which Islam helped the development of medical:

- knowledge
- treatments.

**b** Explain why there was a desire in the Islamic Empire to help the development of medical knowledge and treatments.

**c** Describe in one or two sentences how Islamic medical learning spread to Western Europe after the Early Middle Ages.

**d** Use your answers to parts **a**, **b** and **c** to answer the question: 'Explain the significance of the contribution of Medieval Islam to the development of medicine.'

**EXAMINER TIP**

In your exam, the significance question will require you to explain the short and longer term importance of an event, issue or person. Try to answer this question in relation to the development of medicine in Medieval England.

**REVIEW**

It will help you to assess the contribution of Medieval Islam if you review pages 12–13 and compare with the ideas and attitudes of Medieval Christianity to medicine at the same time.

**FACTORS**

Write down one example of each of the following factors relating to the contribution of Islam to medical progress:

- government
- communication
- role of the individual
- science and technology.

**EXAMINER TIP**

This activity can help you plan for an exam question asking you to decide whether, for example, science and technology was the main factor that led to medical progress in Britain. Note that a Factors question will require you to include information about a range of time periods in your answer.

# Limitations of Medieval surgery

We should not think of Medieval surgery or surgeons in the modern sense. Medieval surgeons learned by watching and copying other surgeons, or on the battlefield.

```
operated without                    had no idea that dirt
effective painkillers               carried disease

            Medieval surgery was
            a risky business for
            the patient because
            surgeons ...

could not help patients             sometimes
with deep wounds to                 thought pus in a
the body                            wound was good
```

Medieval surgical procedures:

- **bloodletting** – frequently to balance the humours
- **amputation** – cutting off of a painful or damaged part of the body e.g. for breast cancer
- **trepanning** – drilling a hole into the skull to 'let the demon out' e.g. for epilepsy
- **cauterisation** – burning a wound to stop the flow of blood using heated iron

A surgeon's toolkit would include saws for amputation, arrow pullers, cautery irons and bloodletting knives. Patients often had to be held or tied down during operations. Natural **anaesthetics** like mandrake root, opium and hemlock were used, but too much might kill the patient.

# Medieval surgical progress and pioneers

In the Medieval period, surgery made some progress in Western Europe and in the Islamic Empire. Surgical pioneers tried new methods. Their books were read in Latin by educated and religious men in Europe. In England, they were translated into English.

### Abulcasis:

- a Muslim surgeon, wrote a 30-volume medical book, *Al Tasrif*, in 1000
- invented 26 new surgical instruments and many new procedures e.g. ligatures
- made cauterisation popular.

### Hugh of Lucca and his son Theodoric:

- in 1267, criticised the common view that pus was needed for a wound to heal
- used wine on wounds to reduce the chances of infection and had new methods of removing arrows
- their ideas to prevent infection clashed with Hippocratic advice and did not become popular.

### Mondino de Luzzi:

- led the new interest in **anatomy** in the fourteenth century
- in 1316, he wrote the book *Anathomia*, which became the standard dissection manual for over 200 years
- in 1315, he supervised a public dissection permitted in Bologna but when the body did not fit Galen's description, the body was thought to be wrong!

### Guy De Chauliac:

- famous French surgeon who wrote influential surgical textbook *Great Surgery* (1363)
- it had many references to Greek and Islamic writers like Avicenna, and quoted Galen about 890 times
- opposed Theodoric of Lucca's ideas about preventing infection; this was the main reason that Lucca's ideas did not catch on.

### John of Arderne:

- the most famous surgeon in Medieval England who set up a 'Guild of Surgeons' in London in 1368
- his surgical manual *Practica* (1376) was based on Greek and Arab knowledge and his experience in the Hundred Years War between England and France
- specialised in operations for anal abscess (swelling with pus), a condition common in knights who spent long periods on horseback.

▼ **SOURCE A** *Abulcasis and his assistant cauterising a mouth wound*

## SUMMARY

- Medieval Islam made great contributions to medical knowledge and valued the medical knowledge of the ancient Greek and Roman world.

- Avicenna wrote the *Canon of Medicine* which became a standard European medical textbook.

- Muslim scientists found new drugs and treatments.

- Muslim medical scholars, like Rhazes and Ibn al-Nafis, were critical of some ancient learning.

- Dissection for learning was banned in Western Europe and Muslim lands.

- Medieval dissections were to demonstrate that Galen was right.

- Medieval surgery was often learned on the battlefield.

- Some surgeons experimented with new ideas, such as using wine to stop infection, but these did not catch on.

- John of Ardenne was the most famous English surgeon of the time.

 **APPLY**

### REVISION SKILLS

Break down the information for a topic in different ways. You can create a brief fact file containing two or three important points about a person or key people.

### SOURCE ANALYSIS

a   What was the most frequently used 'surgery'?

b   How did a Medieval surgeon stop blood flow?

c   Complete a chart about Medieval surgeons and progress. Use the following column headings: Name, Location, Time, Book, Ideas. See the example below.

| Name | Location | Time | Book | Ideas |
|------|----------|------|------|-------|
| Abulcasis | Islamic Empire | 1000 | *Al Tasrif* | New instruments and procedures e.g. cauterisation |

d

 **SOURCE B**  *A fourteenth-century English illustration of a surgeon operating; from a book in a monastic library*

**EXAM QUESTION**  Study **Source B**. How useful is **Source B** to historians studying Medieval surgery?

 **EXAMINER TIP**

If you highlight in your chart the new ideas and practices you will be able to balance the view that the Medieval period was one of no progress.

 **EXAMINER TIP**

Describe what you can see and say why the origin of the source helps a historian understand how medical knowledge was preserved and passed on.

## CHAPTER 3

# Public health in the Middle Ages

**RECAP**

## Public health in Medieval towns

**Public health** is the health and well-being of the population as a whole. Public health in Medieval towns was poor by modern standards, but the hygiene levels were rising in some places:

|  | Unhygienic | Hygienic |
|---|---|---|
| Water | As towns grew, systems could not cope with the increased demand for water; rivers were often used to remove sewage and other waste | Medieval towns took water from local springs, wells or rivers; some Roman systems survived and still worked well while towns like Exeter used new technology with pipes made of wood or lead |
| Sewage | Towns were usually dirty with only a few paved streets; **cesspits** could overflow onto roads and into rivers | Most towns and some private houses had privies (outside toilets) with cesspits to collect the sewage; people left money in their wills to build public privies for the town's citizens |
| Rubbish | In poorer areas streets stank and were often littered with toilet waste and household rubbish | Medieval town councils passed laws encouraging people to keep the streets in front of their houses clean and tidy |
| Tradesmen's waste | Leather tanning used dangerous smelly chemicals while meat butchers dumped the waste blood and guts into rivers | Town councils and local craft guilds tried to encourage tradesmen to keep to certain areas, and keep them clean |

It was difficult to keep Medieval towns clean for a number of reasons.

* Town populations grew and public health facilities couldn't cope.
* Rivers were used for drinking water, for transport, and to remove waste.
* People had no knowledge of germs and their link to disease and infection. They thought that disease was spread by 'bad air', so they were keen to remove unpleasant smells.

Some places had better public health than many towns. Wealthy families could afford better living conditions. But it was in the religious buildings such as monasteries, abbeys and nunneries that the largest number of people enjoyed good public health conditions.

## Conditions in monasteries and abbeys

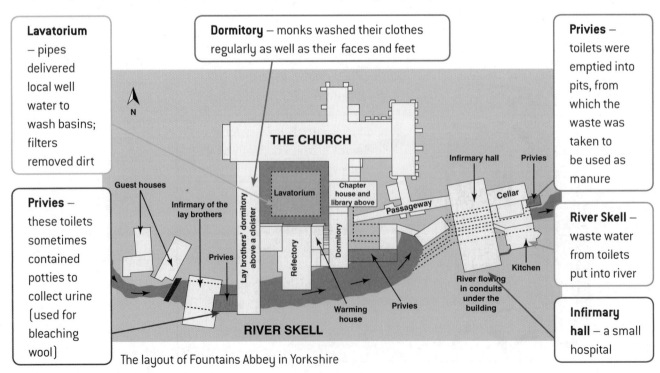

**Lavatorium** – pipes delivered local well water to wash basins; filters removed dirt

**Dormitory** – monks washed their clothes regularly as well as their faces and feet

**Privies** – toilets were emptied into pits, from which the waste was taken to be used as manure

**Privies** – these toilets sometimes contained potties to collect urine (used for bleaching wool)

**River Skell** – waste water from toilets put into river

**Infirmary hall** – a small hospital

The layout of Fountains Abbey in Yorkshire

## Wealth

- money to spend on cleaner facilities
- many people gave money, valuables and lands in return for prayers to be said for them when they died
- monks made a lot of money from producing wool and used the large areas of donated land to keep the sheep

## Knowledge

- monks could read and understand books in their library
- they learned the basic idea of separating clean water from the wastewater that came from the toilets and wash places
- they understood the ancient Roman idea of a simple routine involving moderation in diet, sleep and exercise to balance the humours

## Location

- isolation helped protect monks from **epidemics** (monasteries were usually far away from towns as the Christian Church believed **lay people** were sinful
- Christian monasteries and abbeys were near to rivers; water was an important resource to supply mills, kitchens, bakeries and breweries

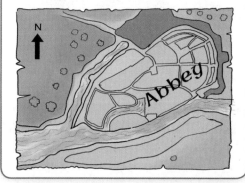

### Why were conditions better?

## Rules

- the monks obeyed the abbot strictly
- they had simple lives that followed a routine
- they kept clean for God and had routines of cleanliness e.g. baths once a month

---

### REVISION SKILLS

Making revision cards is a good way of revising and creating a useful revision aid for later use. Jot down three or four things under a heading on each card. Try to include a factual detail with each point.

## ⚙ APPLY

### FACTORS

a  Why were rivers important for Medieval towns?

b  Make four revision cards covering the following factors about public health in Medieval towns: Town government, Knowledge and attitudes, Wealth and business, Location and facilities.

c  Where did the Fountains Abbey monks obtain their water from?

d  Identify three things that the monks did with their sewage.

e  **EXAM QUESTION** **Was government the main factor that produced better public health in the Middle Ages?**

### EXAMINER TIP

Try to write short paragraphs about some of the other factors— wealth, location and knowledge – as well.

# The Black Death in Britain

The Black Death was a Medieval epidemic disease that arrived in Britain in the mid fourteenth century. It had a major social, economic and political impact on Britain.

- It began in Asia and travelled rapidly along the trade routes to Western Europe.
- It reached Constantinople (in Turkey) in 1347 and arrived in England in 1348.
- It was a combination of **bubonic plague**, spread by rats and fleas, and **pneumonic plague**, which attacked the lungs and was spread by contact with a victim's breath through coughing, or blood.
- Death usually followed a few days after symptoms (lumps or **buboes**, fever and vomiting) were displayed.

| Believed causes | Real causes |
|---|---|
| Position of stars and planets | Bacteria *Yersina Pestis* which grew in fleas' stomachs |
| Bad air | Fleas fed on rats' blood, disease killed rats, fleas moved on to humans |
| Wells poisoned by Jews | Fleas passed the disease on to humans |
| Punishment from God | Food shortages meant the poor were malnourished and more vulnerable to infection |

### Why did the disease spread so quickly?

- **S**treet cleaning was poor.
- **D**irty streets encouraged rats to breed.
- **U**nhygienic habits, e.g. throwing out rubbish, were common.
- **A**nimals dug up quickly-buried victims' bodies.
- **L**aws about cleanliness were difficult to enforce.
- **Q**uarantine was not effective on infected villages.
- **I**gnorance of germs and causes of disease was widespread.

### Remedies

There was no effective cure at the time and in desperation people resorted to the following.

| P | Prayer |
|---|---|
| U | Unusual remedies such as drinking mercury, or shaving a chicken and strapping it to the buboes |
| M | Moving away if they thought the plague was coming |
| A | Avoiding contact with people who might be infected; some local councils tried to **quarantine** infected places |

**REVISION SKILLS**

**Mnemonics** are useful memory devices which can help you recall lists of causes and consequences. There is one here for the remedies – **PUMA**. Can you find another to remind you why the disease spread quickly?

# Major impact on society

The Black Death killed nearly half of Europe's population. In Britain, at least 1.5 million people died between 1348 and 1350.

## Social impact

Whole villages were wiped out

## Political impact

Demands for higher wages contributed to the Peasants' Revolt (1381) and the weakening of the feudal system

## Religious impact

Damage to Catholic Church because experienced priests died; others had run away

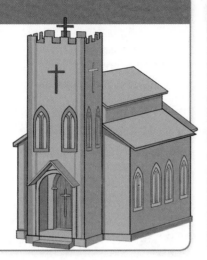

## Economic impact

Plague created food shortages: so the price of food went up, creating more hardship for the poor

Landowners switched to sheep farming as this needed fewer workers

Farm workers demanded higher wages and were less willing to be tied to the land and work for the feudal landlord

## The end of the plague?

- By 1350, the Black Death subsided, but it **never really died out** in England.
- Further outbreaks of the plague occurred at intervals (and with varying degree of deadliness) from the later half of the fourteenth century until the eighteenth century. For example, the plague killed 38,000 Londoners in 1603, and it came again in the **Great Plague of 1665**.

### EXAMINER TIP

It is easy to confuse the dates of the Black Death (which affected England from 1348 to 1350) and the Great Plague of 1665. Try to keep them separate in your mind!

### SUMMARY

- The hygiene in Medieval towns was poor.
- Medieval town councils passed laws to improve cleanliness but could not enforce them.
- Rivers were used for drinking water as well as waste removal.
- Hygiene in monasteries and abbeys was better.
- Conditions in monasteries were better because of their wealth, isolation, and knowledge about hygiene.
- Epidemics like the Black Death flourished in the unhealthy conditions of the towns.
- The Black Death killed half of Europe's population.
- People at the time thought it was a punishment from God and had no effective remedy.
- For those who survived there were great social and economic impacts.

###  APPLY

### REVIEW

To remind yourself of what significance means in history, look at page 15.

### EXPLAIN THE SIGNIFICANCE

a   Identify four ways in which people at the time thought plague was caused.

b   List the reasons why the Black Death was so devastating.

c

> EXAM QUESTION  Explain the significance of the Black Death.

### EXAMINER TIP

Make sure you r● ● different types ● ● e.g. social and economic as well as some longer-term results.

## CHAPTER 4

# The impact of the Renaissance on Britain

 **RECAP**

## The Renaissance

The Renaissance was a cultural movement that began in Florence, Italy, in the late 1400s.

- It began because wealthy businessmen paid scholars and artists to investigate the writings of the ancient Greeks and Romans.
- It inspired people but made them critical of the many versions of old texts; they searched for the most accurate, original versions and experimented with new ideas.
- It made educated people wanted to find out for themselves and not just accept what the Church said.
- It caused a 'rebirth' of learning and a belief that being educated in art, music, science and literature could make life better for everyone.

### The spread of Renaissance

- Before the Renaissance, books were rare and expensive because they were copied out by hand.
- The invention of the printing press in 1451 made books cheap, accurate, and quick to produce.

### The consequences of the Renaissance

**Printing** — new ideas spread quickly as well as those of the ancient world.

**Art** — this showed the human body in realistic detail

**New inventions** — technology such as gunpowder caused new types of wounds.

**New lands** — explorers and merchants used more accurate maps, discovered the Americas and brought back new foods and medicines.

**New learning** — a more scientific approach to learning involving observation, hypothesis, experiment and questioning.

## The work of Vesalius

**Before Vesalius**
- dissections were done to prove Galen was right, not to challenge him
- Galen's words were read while an assistant did the dissection

**Vesalius's work**
- he did the dissections himself
- he said medical students should learn from dissections

**Andreas Vesalius (1514–64)**
- was Belgian and studied in Paris where he learned Galen's anatomy
- as Professor of Surgery at the University of Padua in Italy, he began to question Galen's opinions

**Vesalius's book *The Fabric of the Human Body* (1543)**
- was a beautifully illustrated, very accurate textbook based on dissections and observations of the human body
- corrected Galen's mistakes because he dissected animals
- provided proof of Galen's mistakes, for example the breastbone in a human being has three parts, not seven as in an ape

**Reaction to Vesalius**

- he was criticised for saying Galen was wrong
- he had to leave his job in Padua and later became a doctor for the Emperor Charles V

**Vesalius' contribution to medical progress in England**

- in 1545 Thomas Geminus copied Vesalius' illustrations and put them in a manual for barber-surgeons, called *Compendiosa*
- he added text from de Mondeville's *Surgery* (1312)
- *Compendiosa* was very popular in England, and three editions were published between 1545 and 1559

# Vesalius: an assessment

- Vesalius' work overturned centuries of belief that Galen's study of anatomy was correct.
- His was a Renaissance approach because his work was based on examination of the human body itself.
- Vesalius transformed anatomical knowledge.
- Although Vesalius' work did not lead to any medical cures, it was the basis for better treatments in the future.
- Vesalius showed others how to do proper dissections, and famous sixteenth century anatomists followed his approach, e.g. Fabricius and Fallopius.

**REVIEW**

Galen (131–201) was a famous Greek physician. His books showed observations on the human anatomy. Review Chapters 1 and 2 to remind yourself how Galen's views dominated medical practice and teaching for 1400 years.

## ⚙ APPLY

**SOURCE ANALYSIS**

a Write a definition of the Renaissance as a cultural movement.

b Draw and illustrate a diagram to show what was new about the Renaissance.

c Complete the following 'before' and 'after' table about Vesalius:

| Before | Vesalius | After |
|--------|----------|-------|
| | Textbooks | |
| | Dissection | |
| | Anatomical knowledge | |

d In what ways did Vesalius revolutionise the study of anatomy?

e

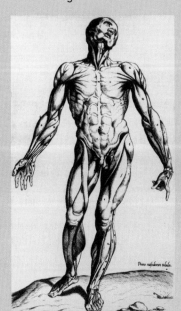

◀ **SOURCE A** *A picture from Thomas Geminus' book* Compendiosa, *first published in England in 1545; three editions had been published by 1549*

**EXAM QUESTION** Study **Source A**. How useful is **Source A** to a historian studying the impact of the Renaissance on Britain?

**REVISION SKILLS**

Memory maps or spider diagrams can be an excellent way of reviewing information. Use colours and small images to make the information memorable.

**EXAMINER TIP**

Note that the date of publication is very close to the publication of *The Fabric of the Human Body* in Italy, and it quickly went through three editions. What does this tell you?

# Renaissance surgery and physiology

**Ambroise Paré** (1510–90) was the most famous Renaissance surgeon in Europe, and published several books about his work. He made several discoveries.

| Before Paré's discoveries | Paré's discoveries | After Paré's discoveries |
|---|---|---|
| Gunshot wounds were thought to be poisonous and were burned out using boiling oil; then a cream of rose oil, egg white and turpentine was applied | 1537 – Paré ran out of hot oil so he improvised and just used the cream<br><br>He challenged accepted practice based on observation and experimentation | Paré's patients' wounds healed well<br><br>He wrote a book about treating wounds (1545) |
| Wounds were cauterised to stop bleeding | Paré used Galen's method of tying blood vessels with **ligatures** or thread<br><br>He invented the **'crow's beak clamp'** to halt bleeding | The ligature was less painful, but was slower and could introduce infection; it also took longer to use in battlefield surgery |
| Paré did many amputations | He designed false limbs for wounded soldiers | He included drawings of the false limbs in his books |

# Paré's contribution to medical progress in England

- Paré translated the work of Andreas Vesalius and used Vesalius's work in his famous *Works on Surgery* (1575).
- This was widely read by English surgeons in the original French, and an English hand-written version appeared in the library of the Barber-Surgeons of London in 1591.
- In sixteenth-century England, Queen Elizabeth I's surgeon William Clowes (1544–1604) made Paré's work well known.
- Clowes, also a battlefield surgeon, described Paré as the 'famous surgeon master'.
- He copied Paré's burn treatment using onions in 1596.
- Like Paré he said that gunshot wounds were not poisonous and wrote about stopping bleeding from wounds in his book *Proved Practice* (1588).

# Harvey's contribution to medical progress

William Harvey (1578–1657) was an English doctor who challenged Galen by saying the blood circulated round the body

Galen said new blood was constantly made in the liver and burned as a fuel in the body

## Harvey's discovery of the circulation of the blood

- He **calculated** mathematically how much blood would have to be produced if it was a fuel for the body.

- He **observed** the slow-beating hearts of cold-blooded animals to understand how the muscles worked.
- He **read** widely what the Italian anatomists at Padua discovered, and built upon their work.
- He **dissected** and studied human hearts.
- He **experimented** pumping liquid the wrong way through valves in the veins, proving that blood could only go round one way.

## What did Harvey not know?

Harvey waited 12 years before publishing *De Motu Cordis* (1628) about the circulation of the blood! There were several reasons.

| Harvey did not know: | But he did know there would be criticism: |
|---|---|
| why the blood circulated | of his going against Galen |
| why there was different coloured blood in the arteries and veins | of his challenging the idea of bloodletting to balance the humours |
| how the blood got from the arteries to the veins | |

## Reactions to Harvey's discovery

Harvey's critics said he was mad, or ignored his ideas. Some doctors rejected his theory because he was contradicting Galen, or did not believe his calculations.

Despite all the criticism, Harvey's theory was accepted by many doctors. It wasn't until 1661, four years after Harvey died, that a good enough microscope was made to see the capillaries connecting veins and arteries.

### EXAMINER TIP

It is important for you to understand why there was opposition to Harvey's discovery. It was partly based on what he did not know!

## The significance of Harvey's discovery

Harvey's discovery was not immediately useful. Transfusions did not happen until 1901, when blood groups were discovered. Today, understanding the blood and its circulation is significant because it allows us to quickly test and diagnose illness, and to carry out advanced surgery like organ transplants.

### SUMMARY

- The Renaissance was a movement that questioned old accepted ideas.

- Printing was very important for spreading Renaissance ideas.

- Vesalius dissected human bodies himself, and made and recorded his discoveries which showed how Galen was wrong.

- Vesalius's work was quickly copied by others such as Thomas Geminus in England.

- Paré developed new surgical techniques.

- Harvey used scientific methods to discover the circulation of the blood but the idea met much opposition.

## ⚙ APPLY

### FACTORS

a  Identify two improvements in surgery that Paré made.

b  How did William Clowes make Paré's work widely known in England?

c  Summarise Galen's beliefs about blood.

d  Identify two things about Harvey's methods that show him as a good scientist.

e  **EXAM QUESTION**  Was printing the main feature of medicine during the Renaissance?

### EXAMINER TIP

You will be able to use Paré as an example of a Renaissance figure who made discoveries through challenging existing ideas.

### EXAMINER TIP

A plan for your answer could be:

- a paragraph about medical books

- a paragraph about overcoming opposition

- a paragraph about the critical, scientific approach of Renaissance medicine.

### REVIEW

You should look back at pages 22–23 to remind yourself about the main features of the Renaissance and Vesalius.

### REVISION SKILLS

For longer questions always plan your answer. Aim to write three paragraphs and a conclusion. Jot down a few points to give a shape to your answer. Practise planning answers to questions.

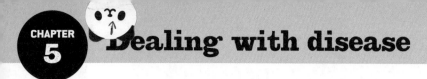

# CHAPTER 5 Dealing with disease

 **RECAP**

## Traditional and new treatments

Medical ideas and beliefs in the seventeenth and eighteenth centuries were a mixture of traditional and new, more scientific treatments, as the work of Nicholas Culpeper and Thomas Sydenham shows.

| Nicholas Culpeper | Thomas Sydenham (1624–89) |
|---|---|
| Wrote *The complete herbal* (1653) <br><br> Used plants and astrology in his treatments <br><br> Highly critical of bloodletting and purging | English doctor who stressed the careful observation of symptoms and was critical of quack medicine <br><br> Noted the symptoms of scarlet fever, and used iron for treating anaemia <br><br> Dismissed the value of dissections and ignored Harvey's discovery because it did not help in treating patients <br><br> Still used bleeding methods for treatment <br><br> His book *Medical Observations* (1676) became a standard textbook |

**Treatments:**

- bloodletting
- herbal remedies, for example new natural medicines such as the bark of the Cinchona tree from South America which contained quinine for malaria
- opium from Turkey used as an anaesthetic
- the discovery by the military surgeon, John Woodall in 1617, of lemons and limes to treat scurvy
- beliefs, such as the power of the royal touch to cure the disease scrofula, or 'king's evil'

**REVISION SKILLS**

Create a ten-point fact test to check detailed knowledge about these traditional and new medical ideas. You can swap tests with a friend.

## Medical treatment in the seventeenth and eighteenth centuries

These came from a number of sources and depended on what you could afford.

- **Barber-surgeons**: poorly trained people who would give you a haircut and perhaps perform a small operation like bloodletting or tooth pulling.

- **Apothecaries**: they had little or no medical training, but sold medicines and potions.

- **Wise women**: their treatments often relied on superstition. However, they often had extensive knowledge of plants and herbs.

- **Quacks**: showy, travelling salesmen who sold all sorts of medicines and 'cure-alls'.

- **Trained doctors**: such as those who treated Charles II using a mixture of new and traditional knowledge including the four humours.

## The Great Plague

In 1665 the plague returned in an epidemic that killed about 100,000 people in London (around a quarter of the city's population) and thousands of people in the rest of the country.

**REVIEW**

Remind yourself of what people thought caused the Black Death; they had some of the same ideas in 1665.

Remedies and treatments at the time included the following:

- bleeding with leeches

- smoking to keep away the 'poisoned' air

- sniffing a sponge soaked in vinegar

- using animals such as frogs, pigeons, snakes and scorpions to 'draw out the poison'

- moving to the countryside to avoid catching the plague, as King Charles II and the court did.

### Dealing with the Great Plague: what had people learned since the Black Death?

People recognised the likely **connection between dirt and the disease**; most deaths occurred in the poorest, dirtiest areas.

There was a **more organised approach** this time. Mayors and councillors issued orders to try to halt the spread of the disease.

'Women searchers' **identified plague victims**, examined the sick, and noted those with plague symptoms.

There was **more effective quarantine** (locking up) of victims in their houses, guarded by watchmen.

Bodies were removed at night and **buried in mass plague pits**.

**Fires were lit** to try to remove the poisons that were thought to be in the air.

Orders were issued for **streets to be swept** and animals were not allowed in the streets.

**Gatherings of crowds** for plays or games were banned.

**Trade between plague towns stopped** and the Scottish border closed.

## How did the plague end?

- It was not true that the Great Fire of London in 1666 ended the plague by burning down the poor housing. The fire destroyed houses within the city walls. The poorest areas, where most of the plague deaths happened, were outside the city walls.

- The plague declined because the rats developed a greater resistance to the disease, and so their fleas did not need to find human hosts.

- After 1666, quarantine laws prevented epidemic diseases coming into the country on ships.

### ⚙ APPLY

**SIMILARITY**

a Study the table at the top of page 26. Highlight in two colours treatments that were new and treatments that were traditional.

b Construct a spider diagram to show how people dealt with the Great Plague.

c **EXAM QUESTION** Explain two ways in which treatments in the Middle Ages and treatments in the seventeenth and eighteenth centuries were similar.

**EXAMINER TIP** ⊚

You could refer to the treatments, the sources of medical advice, and reactions to epidemics like the Black Death.

# Scientific medicine in the seventeenth and eighteenth centuries

In the seventeenth and eighteenth centuries the practice of scientific medicine in modern hospitals began. These hospitals were paid for either by the rich, such as Guy's Hospital in London (1724), or by 'private subscription', where local people clubbed together to pay.

## Hospitals in the eighteenth century

- Many new hospitals were built; 1720–50 saw five new general hospitals built in London.

- Patient numbers increased; London's hospitals had over 20,000 patients a year by 1800.

- Hospitals had specialist wards for different types of disease, and often had medical schools to train doctors.

- Hospital treatment was free but still mainly based on the four humours approach of bleeding and purging.

- Attitudes to illness changed as more Christians thought it better to help the sick than to argue about beliefs and types of church service.

- Fewer people thought illness was a punishment for sin. Instead they thought that illness could be dealt with by a more evidence-based, scientific approach.

- Towards the end of the eighteenth century, some hospitals added pharmacies, giving the poor free medicines, such as in Edinburgh (1776).

- Specialist hospitals grew up such as London's Lock Hospital for venereal disease (1746) and a maternity hospital, the British Hospital for Mothers and Babies (1749).

## John Hunter

John Hunter (1728–93) was a pioneer of scientific surgery. He was appointed Surgeon to King George III in 1776, and Surgeon-General to the army in 1790.

### Hunter's books

- Based on his observations, dissection skill, and experimentation, as well as his experience in the army. Example are *The Natural History of the Teeth* (1771), *On Venereal Disease* (1786), and *Blood inflammation and gunshot wounds* (1794)
- Included his discoveries about the nature of disease, cancer, and the circulation of the blood, with recommendations such as not enlarging gunshot wounds when treating them

### Hunter's collection

- Collected and studied 3000 anatomical specimens such as stuffed animals, dried plants, fossils, diseased organs, and embryos
- Experimented by pumping wax into blood vessels to study circulation

### Hunter's methods

- Demanded careful observation in surgery; experimented on himself in 1767, with gonorrhoea germs
- Tried radical surgery; in 1785 he saved a man's leg with a throbbing lump (aneurysm) on his knee joint, instead of performing the usual amputation

### Hunter's teaching

- Taught hundreds of other surgeons (such as Edward Jenner) in his scientific approach
- Inspired many young surgeons to become great medical teachers and professors, some of whom founded famous teaching hospitals in nineteenth-century Britain and America

## SUMMARY

- Treatments in the seventeenth and eighteenth centuries were a mixture of traditional and new, more scientific, treatments.

- In dealing with the Great Plague some of the measures taken would have helped but people were still no nearer explaining the epidemic.

- Hospitals in the eighteenth century were better organised and directed at curing rather than simply caring for sick people.

- Some hospitals were specialised and doctors could train at them.

- John Hunter founded a scientific approach to surgery.

## APPLY

### SOURCE ANALYSIS

**a** Who paid for eighteenth-century hospitals to be built?

**b** Identify four things about eighteenth-century hospitals that were new.

**c** Give an example of how John Hunter challenged traditional views.

**d** Identify one piece of supporting evidence for each of the following factors in John Hunter's career: warfare, individual ability, scientific method, communication.

**e**

 **SOURCE A** *A painting of John Hunter, completed in 1813 by the famous English portrait painter, John Jackson*

> **EXAM QUESTION** Study **Source A**. How useful is **Source A** to a historian studying the development of anatomy?

### REVISION SKILLS

Reducing information to a shorter, more concise form is valuable. After reading a couple of pages of a textbook or your notes, ask yourself, 'What are the six most important things I need to remember?' Write these down on a piece of paper or small card. Don't worry about the things that you have left behind on the page – you will remember those next time!

## CHAPTER 6

# Prevention of disease

## RECAP

## Edward Jenner and the prevention of smallpox

**Smallpox** was one of the most feared diseases of the eighteenth century.

**Smallpox facts**

- one of the biggest killer diseases in the eighteenth century
- a highly infectious virus spread by the coughing, sneezing or touching of an infected person
- killed 30 per cent of those who caught it

**Prevention**

- using **inoculation**
- but this was controversial and didn't always work

**Symptoms**

- fever, headache and a rash
- followed by pus-filled blisters covering the entire body
- even if you survived, you could be left blind or with deep scars

**SOURCE A** *A painting, from 1823, of a man being shown his face affected by smallpox*

## Jenner's discovery of vaccination

Cowpox is a milder version of smallpox that usually affected cows. Edward Jenner (1749–1823) was a country doctor in Gloucestershire. Jenner may have heard stories that people catching cowpox were protected against smallpox. He decided to test this theory in 1796 by giving cowpox to an eight-year-old boy as an experiment. If the cowpox was to work, then the child would not react to the follow-up smallpox inoculation; if it was to fail, then the boy would develop smallpox scabs in the normal way. Six weeks later, he gave the boy smallpox inoculation: no disease followed.

Jenner called his cowpox inoculation technique **vaccination**, based on the Latin word for cow (*vacca*). Jenner repeated the experiment over several weeks with 16 different patients. None of them reacted to smallpox inoculation. Jenner concluded correctly that cowpox protected humans from smallpox.

## Inoculation

- It involved giving a healthy person a mild dose of the disease. Dried scabs were scratched into their skin or blown up their nose. It allowed them to build up resistance against the deadly version.
- It became fashionable after 1721 when, having seen it done in Turkey, Lady Mary Wortley Montagu had her children inoculated.
- It became common from the 1740s and many doctors became rich from the procedure.

### The problems with inoculation

- Some people had religious objections, believing that preventing sickness interfered with God's will.
- There was a lack of understanding, and disbelief that it would work.
- There was a risk that the smallpox dose was not mild, and could kill.
- Inoculated people could still pass on smallpox to others.
- Poor people could not afford to be inoculated.

## Reasons for opposition to Jenner and vaccination

Jenner published his findings in 1798 but …

- he could not explain how vaccination worked
- many doctors were profiting from smallpox inoculation
- attempts to repeat his experiment failed; for example in the London Smallpox Hospital, William Woodville and George Pearson tested cowpox, but their equipment was contaminated and a patient died
- Jenner was not a fashionable city doctor, so there was snobbery against him.

## Why was vaccination accepted?

Vaccination became accepted because …

- Jenner had proved the effectiveness of vaccination by scientific experiment
- vaccination was less dangerous than inoculation
- members of the royal family were vaccinated, which influenced opinion
- Parliament acknowledged Jenner's research with a £10,000 grant in 1802
- in 1853 the British government made smallpox vaccination compulsory.

---

**SUMMARY**

- Smallpox was the biggest killer of the eighteenth century.

- Inoculation was the usual way to prevent smallpox, but it carried risks.

- Jenner tested whether cowpox vaccination was a better way to prevent smallpox.

- Cowpox vaccination worked, but when Jenner published his findings in 1798 there was opposition.

---

 **APPLY**

**REVISION SKILLS**

Break down the information for a topic in different ways. You can create a timeline with five or six dates.

**EXPLAIN THE SIGNIFICANCE**

**a** Describe briefly Jenner's experiment.

**b** Explain why catching smallpox terrified people.

**c** Complete a copy of the table below to compare inoculation and vaccination.

|  | Inoculation | Vaccination |
|---|---|---|
| Definition |  |  |
| When popular |  |  |
| Problems and drawbacks |  |  |
| Celebrity/royal endorsement |  |  |

**d**  EXAM QUESTION  Explain the significance of Jenner's work with vaccination.

**EXAMINER TIP**

Jenner's work can be seen as significant for the role of the British government.

## CHAPTER 7

# Advances in medical science in nineteenth-century Britain

 **RECAP**

## The problem of pain

- In 1800, surgery was a terrifying prospect because surgeons could not control or stop pain during an operation.
- Before 1800, there were some pain deadening substances that had been known for centuries, such as hashish, mandrake and opium. But it was difficult to judge an effective dose.
- Alcohol was used but it stimulated the heart and caused heavy bleeding in a wound.
- The result was that surgeons had to operate quickly to reduce pain and would not attempt complicated internal surgery.

### New anaesthetics: chemistry to the rescue!

**Nitrous oxide**: an account published by Humphrey Davy in 1800 described its effects — hysterical laughter and no pain. Not used until 1844 when the American dentist Horace Wells used it to remove teeth.

**Ether**: in 1842, William Clark, another American dentist, used ether for tooth extraction and in March that year, Dr Crawford Long removed a neck growth from a patient using it. In 1846, William Morton gave a public demonstration of ether anaesthesia. In December 1846, Robert Liston amputated a leg using it. But it was difficult to inhale, caused vomiting, and was highly flammable.

**Chloroform**: a safe and effective anaesthetic, discovered by Dr James Simpson in 1847.

## The reasons for the opposition to anaesthetics

Surgeons were used to operating quickly and on a conscious patient.

Some army surgeons during the Crimean War (1853–56) thought that soldiers should dutifully put up with the pain.

In the early days of using chloroform, some patients died because it was not understood that patients of different sizes needed different amounts of chloroform. Famously, Hannah Greener died from an overdose in 1848 during an operation to remove her toenail.

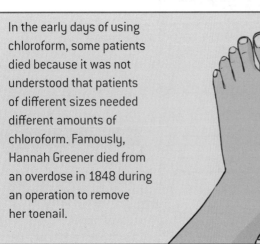

There were religious objections as pain in childbirth was thought to be God's will.

# Objections overcome

- In 1853, Queen Victoria used anaesthetics for childbirth which made it acceptable and fashionable.
- However, anaesthetics did not revolutionise surgery because there was still a high death rate from infections introduced by operations.

### REVISION SKILLS

Record yourself reading your notes. Playback the information when you are travelling, or waiting.

### SIMILARITY

**a** What were the problems with pain relief before 1800?

_____

_____

_____

_____

_____

**b** Organise the following dates and people into a timeline:

| 1846 | Hannah Greener |
| 1848 | Crawford Long |
| 1842 | Queen Victoria |
| 1844 | James Simpson |
| 1847 | Horace Wells |
| 1853 | Robert Liston |

**c** Copy and complete the table below of the reasons for opposition to vaccination and anaesthetics.

| Vaccination | Reason for opposition | Anaesthetics |
|---|---|---|
| Preferred inoculation | Doctors didn't like it | Wanted to work quickly |
| | | |
| | | |

**REVIEW**

You may need to remind yourself about the reasons why the vaccination was opposed by reading pages 30–31.

**d** **EXAM QUESTION** Explain two ways in which the opposition to vaccination and the opposition to using anaesthetics were similar.

**EXAMINER TIP**

Identify the similarity first, and then write about the evidence for it specifically, from both topics. Try to find at least two points of similarity.

# Early nineteenth-century ideas about infection

Surgery carried a high risk of infection. Surgeons believed that chemicals in the wound caused the infection, but they were puzzled why some deep wounds healed quickly, and other surface scratches proved fatal. Surgeons tried to keep the patient healthy and the wound clean. If it became infected, they used cauterising or acids to burn away the affected tissues.

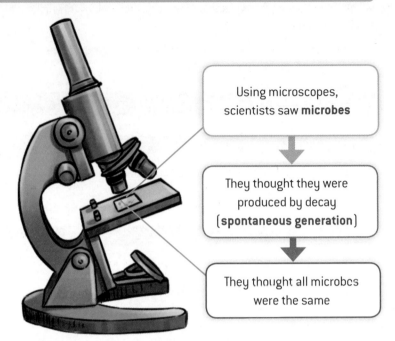

Using microscopes, scientists saw **microbes**

↓

They thought they were produced by decay (**spontaneous generation**)

↓

They thought all microbes were the same

## Challenging spontaneous generation

Spontaneous generation was questioned in the debate about public health.

| Contagionists | Anti-contagionists |
|---|---|
| Believed infection was spread by contact and could be controlled by quarantine | Believed infection was caused by the environment: epidemics such as cholera could be controlled by cleaning |
| In 1864, surgeon Thomas Wells first suggested infection was non-chemical and referred to Pasteur's discoveries | Doctors like James Simpson wanted hospitals relocated or rebuilt as they thought infection was in their walls or the atmosphere (**miasma**) |

# Louis Pasteur's Germ Theory

Pasteur proved that spontaneous generation was wrong and that germs, not chemicals, caused decay.

# Germ Theory in Britain: Joseph Lister

In the late 1860s, Pasteur's Germ Theory came to the attention of British doctors, and revolutionised surgery because of the work of Joseph Lister (1827–1912).

Lister was a Professor of Surgery in Glasgow, and was shown Pasteur's research by Thomas Anderson, a Professor of Chemistry. Lister thought that Pasteur's Germ Theory might explain surgical infection. Anderson also recommended carbolic acid as a chemical that killed bacteria.

▼ **SOURCE A** *The French scientist, Louis Pasteur, carrying out the swan-necked flask experiment to show how liquids go off when exposed to the air; his work was published in 1861 and proved that bacteria were the real reason why things decayed*

## Lister and the antiseptic approach

- Spray carbolic acid on the surgeon's hands and operating area
- Soak the instruments and bandages in carbolic acid
- In August 1865, he mended the fractured leg of a young boy, Jamie Greenlees
- As the skin of Jamie's leg was broken it was likely to be infected and usually would be amputated
- Instead, Lister set the bones and used dressings that had been soaked in carbolic acid
- After six weeks, Jamie walked out of hospital

## Lister's conclusion

- In 1867, Lister published the results of 11 cases of compound fracture, explained his techniques in lectures, and publicised Pasteur's Germ Theory through his explanation of the antiseptic technique
- Lister said that the microbes in the air caused the infection, not spontaneous generation

## Reactions to Lister's work in Britain

- Lister's ideas were criticised
- The public health debate focused on chemical causes of infection
- Lister's biological explanation was unfamiliar
- British surgeons offered alternative explanations
- Spontaneous generation was supported by influential doctors like Charlton Bastian

# Reasons for opposition to antiseptic surgery

- Doctors at the time did not accept Pasteur's Germ Theory and the role of microbes in wounds.
- In the late 1860s, antiseptic chemicals had been widely used. Lister's methods were not revolutionary even though he claimed they were superior.
- Carbolic acid dried skin and irritated lungs, and it took nurses a long time for to prepare his carbolic methods.
- Lister changed his techniques and surgeons said this was due to ineffectiveness.
- In the 1870s, Lister still believed microbes were very simple things and that there might be only one type that caused disease.
- He only rinsed his hands in carbolic acid and still operated in his street clothes.

## REVISION SKILLS

Having someone test you on your notes and revision is an excellent way of seeing how much you remember, understand, and still have to learn. Brief oral test sessions of about 10 minutes are best.

##  APPLY

### SIMILARITY

a  What did scientists believe about microbes in the early nineteenth century?

b  How did doctors explain the germs they found in wounds?

c  Make five revision cards with the following headings: Lister's inspiration; Lister's experiment; Lister's methods; Lister's conclusions; Lister's critics.

d  **EXAM QUESTION** Explain two ways in which opposition to Lister's antiseptic methods and opposition to Harvey's discovery of the circulation of the blood were similar.

### REVIEW

Look back to pages 24–25 to remind yourself about William Harvey.

### EXAMINER TIP

One similarity is that both did scientific experiments. Explain the way in which both men were good scientists.

# Louis Pasteur and the Germ Theory debate

Despite Lister's attempts to convince British surgeons that Pasteur's Germ Theory explained infections, various theories were still debated in the 1860s and 1870s.

- Most doctors at the time still did not believe that microscopic germs could harm something as large and advanced as a human.

- Louis Pasteur's research related to specific germs that might turn liquid foods – such as milk – sour, or give diseases to animals. It did not relate to those that might make people ill.

- An influential doctor, Charlton Bastian, Professor of Anatomy at University College London, had written many articles in the late 1860s that supported spontaneous generation. Many did not want to challenge his views.

# Why did people begin to change their minds?

### The cattle plague of 1866

Initially it was believed that the disease started spontaneously. Farmers were reluctant to kill cattle so the disease spread quickly nationwide. When vets imposed quarantines and the slaughter of cattle, the disease was halted. The government appointed a scientist, Professor Lionel Beale, who used the latest microscopes and identified the specific microbe responsible. The cattle plague was clearly spread by contact.

### John Tyndall

Famous physicist John Tyndall argued in favour of Germ Theory and against the influential Charlton Bastian. He lectured on dust and disease, demonstrating the existence of tiny microbes in ordinary air.

### Typhoid fever

Typhoid was common throughout Britain. Anti-contagionists said that all that was needed was to clean up the towns. In 1876, the German scientist Robert Koch's work identified specific germs that caused particular diseases such as cholera and typhoid. John Tyndall lectured doctors about Koch's work.

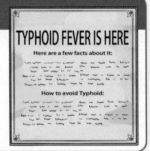

# Aseptic surgery

By the 1880s, British doctors had accepted Germ Theory and its role in explaining infection. By the 1890s, surgeons in Europe and North America went beyond Lister's antiseptic methods and developed **aseptic** surgery, aiming to remove microbes before an operation began rather than kill them as it progressed.

Surgeons had to be scrubbed, wearing gowns and new, thin flexible gloves, and using sterilised instruments. The first British surgeon to use rubber gloves was Berkeley Moynihan in the 1890s. Facemasks, rubber gloves, surgical gowns, and replacing huge public operating theatres with smaller rooms dramatically reduced infections.

## SUMMARY

- In 1800, there was no effective pain relief during surgery. Therefore surgeons had to operate quickly.

- In 1847, James Simpson found an effective safe anaesthetic – chloroform.

- Opposition to the use of anaesthetics was overcome when Queen Victoria used it in childbirth.

- The risk of infection from surgery remained until Louis Pasteur's Germ Theory was accepted.

- Joseph Lister publicised Germ Theory through his use of carbolic acid to kill bacteria during surgery.

- Many doctors did not accept that germs caused disease: they thought germs were the product of disease and occurred through spontaneous generation.

- Surgeons opposed Lister's methods as they disliked the fuss of using carbolic acid, preferred to work quickly, and had their own methods to deal with infection.

- Germ Theory was advanced by the 1866 cattle plague which proved that one microbe could cause illness by contact.

- The theory was further advanced by John Tyndall, who argued against Charlton Bastian about spontaneous generation, and by Robert Koch's work on cholera and typhoid.

## REVISION SKILLS

Write facts on notes and stick them up together in a specific part of your room or house. When you go or look there you will read your notes and associate that part of the room or house with this topic.

##  APPLY

## FACTORS

**a** How did the cattle plague of 1866 help to prove Germ Theory?

**b** Koch's work on typhoid germs proved the anti-contagionists wrong. How?

**c** Rather than killing germs present during surgery, what does aseptic surgery try to do?

**d**  EXAM QUESTION  Was Lister's antiseptic method the main factor in bringing about the acceptance of Germ Theory in Britain?

### EXAMINER TIP

It will help if you have read page 38 before you tackle part **d**. William Roberts and William Cheney also helped the acceptance of Germ Theory in Britain.

## REVISION SKILLS

Make sure you know the question types you will be asked in each part of the examination. Find out how many marks there are for each type of question.

## CHAPTER 8

# Further impact of Germ Theory in Britain

 **RECAP**

## Robert Koch

**Robert Koch** was a German doctor who applied Pasteur's Germ Theory to human diseases. He was the founder of bacteriology – the study of bacteria.

- His work went against the view that most germs were very similar.
- He identified the microbe responsible for anthrax in 1876.
- He identified the deadly cholera germs in 1884 and tuberculosis germs in 1882.

### Robert Koch's methods

- He proved that specific bacteria were responsible for a specific disease by injecting and retrieving the bacterium from successive experimental animals.
- He improved the growing of microbes on solidified agar (a seaweed extract).
- He discovered dyes to stain specific microbes so they stood out under a microscope.
- He perfected a lens to photograph microbes, allowing other scientists to recognise them.
- Koch's team helped to train many young scientists to use his methods.

## Germ Theory accepted in Britain, 1870s

- Microscope research was conducted into the life cycle of germs by scientists William Dallinger and John Drysdale in 1874.
- John Tyndall continued to lecture British doctors on Koch's discoveries.
- Dr William Roberts developed a medical version of the Germ Theory of disease.
- In 1879, the surgeon William Cheyne translated Koch's work and explained how the microbes present in wounds did not always produce disease.

**War**

France and Germany were rivals because France had lost a war against Germany in 1871

**Government and finance**

Both Pasteur and Koch had a laboratory and a scientific team paid for by their governments

**Teamwork**

Between 1880 and 1884, Pasteur and his team developed a vaccine for rabies; in 1885 they proved it worked on humans as well as animals by saving a young boy

**Factors in the struggle to develop vaccines**

**Individual character**

Pasteur was a determined scientist despite suffering a stroke and losing his daughter to typhoid

Between 1876 and 1881, Pasteur was motivated by Koch's success identifying anthrax

**Competition**

From 1888 to 1890, there was research rivalry over diphtheria; one of Pasteur's scientists, Pierre Roux, showed that the diphtheria germ produced a poison or toxin

In 1890, Emil Behring, one of Koch's students, showed that weakened diphtheria germs could produce an antitoxin

(4) The disease affects the second animal; bacteria are taken from this animal

(2a) The bacteria are grown in a pure culture

(5a) Disease–causing bacteria are grown in a pure culture

(3) The bacteria are injected into a healthy animal

(1) Bacteria are taken from a dead animal

(5b) Identical bacteria are identified

(2b) The bacteria are identified

▲ **Koch's laboratory method**

## Communication

Pasteur's vaccine against anthrax was demonstrated publicly to an audience of politicians, farmers and journalists in France in May 1881; news of it spread by electric telegraph

## Luck

In 1879, the accidental use of weakened chicken cholera germs gave the chickens immunity when injected with fresh strong germs; Pasteur had inadvertently shown how vaccines could give immunity and prevent disease

# Impact of Pasteur's and Koch's work in Britain

- Pasteur and Koch encouraged a new generation of scientists to study deadly diseases and to find ways of preventing them.

- Joseph Lister used the diphtheria antitoxin in Britain and by 1905 the death rate was halved.

- By the 1880s, British doctors accepted Germ Theory but deep inside the body they could not use intense heat or powerful antiseptics.

- However, scientists found chemicals that attacked specific germs. In 1909, Paul Ehrlich (a former member of Koch's team) developed the first chemical cure for a disease, Salvarsan 606, which cured syphilis.

## SUMMARY

- Robert Koch was a German doctor who applied Pasteur's Germ Theory to human diseases.

- He identified specific germs that caused human diseases.

- He provided bacteriologists with the tools to identify specific germs.

- Germ Theory was accepted in the 1870s because of the arguments of John Tyndall against Charlton Bastian, who advocated spontaneous generation.

- Tyndall was backed up by other British scientists and doctors such as William Roberts and William Cheyne, who explained medically how Germ Theory caused infection.

- Pasteur and Koch were rivals, gaining fame for their countries, France and Germany, through scientific discoveries.

## ⚙ APPLY

### SOURCE ANALYSIS

▼ **SOURCE A** *A cartoon called 'Koch as the new St George', from an English newspaper in the 1880s; it shows Koch conquering the bacteria responsible for tuberculosis*

a   Construct a spider diagram for all the factors involved in the development of vaccines between 1880 and 1900. Use two colours to highlight Pasteur's and Koch's contributions.

b   Make a fact file about Robert Koch. List his methods and discoveries.

c    Study **Source A**. How useful is **Source A** to a historian studying the importance of Robert Koch?

## CHAPTER 9

# Improvements in public health

RECAP

## Cholera and public health

There were great changes to the way people lived and worked in Britain in the late eighteenth and nineteenth centuries. This had a major impact on public health.

### Industrialisation

- Britain's cities grew quickly from 1800. For example, Sheffield's population of just 12,000 people in 1750 was over 150,000 by 1850.

- Thousands of people moved from the countryside to cities like London, Sheffield, Birmingham, Leeds and Manchester to work in the new factories of the Industrial Revolution.

### Conditions in the cities

- A single factory would employ hundreds of people, so factory owners quickly built rows of 'back-to-back' houses.

- Many workers were squeezed into each house, often with five or more people living in one small room.

- Few of the houses had toilets; most were outside and shared with other families.

- Water for drinking and cooking came from a pump fed by the local pond or river, which would also take away sewage.

- There were no rubbish collections, no street cleaners or sewers, and no fresh running water.

▼ **SOURCE A** *A diagram adapted from evidence given to a government inquiry into the 'State of the Large Towns', 1844. It shows back-to-back housing in Nottingham*

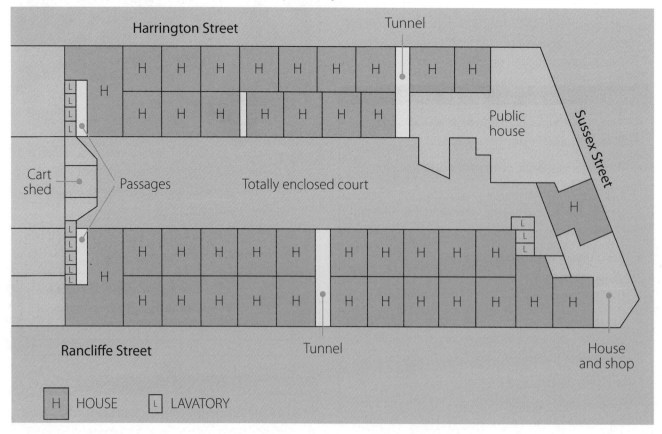

## Health problems in the cities

- As a result of the poor living conditions and overcrowding, diseases like typhoid, tuberculosis and cholera were common.
- In 1831, a cholera outbreak killed around 50,000 people. Victims were violently sick and suffered from painful diarrhoea before dying.
- There were further cholera epidemics in 1837, 1838, 1848, 1853–54 and 1865–66.
- Cholera was a waterborne disease but at this time many believed it was spread through the air, as a miasma or 'infectious mist' given off by rubbish and human waste.
- This led some towns to clean up their streets; the importance of clean drinking water wasn't understood.
- Governments in all major European nations were concerned about epidemics but they did not know how to deal with them.
- A link had been made between the poor living conditions and the rising death rate – but in the early 1800s people did not know what really caused disease.

# Some of the most common diseases of the 1800s

| Disease | Cause | Description |
|---|---|---|
| Typhoid | Contaminated water or food | Spread by poor sanitation or unhygienic conditions; sewage would get into the water supply that people drank |
| Tuberculosis (TB) | Germs passed in the air through sneezing or coughing | Spread rapidly in crowded areas; another type of TB was caused by infected cows' milk |
| Cholera | Contaminated water or food | Several cholera epidemics swept the country in the early 1800s |

 APPLY

### SOURCE ANALYSIS

a  Why did towns grow so quickly in the late 1700s and early 1800s?

b  Make revision cards about public health during the Industrial Revolution. Use the following headings: water supply, toilets, housing, street cleaning and disease.

c  **EXAM QUESTION** Study **Source A**. How useful is **Source A** for understanding how disease spread in the 1800s?

**EXAMINER TIP**

Try to link what you can see in the source with your own knowledge of life in industrial towns at this time.

### REVISION SKILLS

Making revision cards is a good way of revising and creating a useful revision aid for later use. Jot down three or four things under a heading on each card. Try to include a factual detail with each point.

 **RECAP**

# Governments and public health in the nineteenth century

After cholera outbreaks in 1837 and 1838, the government set up an inquiry into living conditions and the health of the poor. They put Edwin Chadwick in charge.

Chadwick's report, published in 1842, shocked Britain. Twenty thousand copies were sold to the public. Although Chadwick believed in the mistaken miasma theory, his report clearly highlighted the need for cleaner streets and clean water.

## Chadwick's report – key points

- Disease is caused by bad air, damp, filth, and by overcrowded houses. When these things are improved, the death rate goes down.

- Medical officers should be appointed to take charge in each district.

- People cannot develop clean habits until they have clean water.

- A healthier workforce would work harder and cost the rich less in the long run.

- Laws should be passed to improve drainage and sewers, funded by local taxpayers.

## Reactions to Chadwick's report

- The government did not act on Chadwick's report because it believed in 'laissez-faire' ideas that said it was not their job to interfere in people's lives and force them to be hygienic.

- MPs who rented out slum houses did not want the expense of having to tear them down and rebuild them.

## Action at last

- There was another cholera epidemic in 1848 (killing nearly 60,000 people). The government decided to act at last, and passed a law – the 1848 Public Health Act.
- A Central Board of Health was set up to improve public health in towns.
- Any town could set up its own Local Board of Health (but this was not compulsory).
- Local town councils were empowered to spend money on cleaning up their streets.
- Some towns, such as Liverpool, Sunderland and Birmingham, made huge improvements, but other cities chose to do nothing.
- By 1853, only 103 towns had set up a Local Board of Health, and in 1854 the Central Board of Health was closed down because government interference was strongly resented.

# Dr Snow links cholera to contaminated water

- During another cholera outbreak in 1854, 20,000 people died. Dr John Snow noted that all the victims lived near the same water pump in Broad Street, Soho, London. He removed the pump handle and so everyone had to use another water pump. The outbreak stopped.

- Snow later found that a street toilet was leaking into the pump's water source. Snow suspected that cholera was not airborne (miasma), but contagious and caught by contact with infected water.

## The Great Stink

- Despite Snow's findings, public health didn't improve. City streets and water supplies remained as filthy as ever.
- In the summer of 1858, a heat wave caused the filthy River Thames to produce the 'Great Stink'.
- This alarmed politicians so much that, combined with the new evidence about cholera, they agreed to pay for sanitary improvements.
- Parliament gave the engineer Joseph Bazalgette enough money to build a new sewer system for London. By 1866, he had built an 83-mile sewer system which removed 420 million gallons of sewage a day.

▼ **SOURCE A** *A cartoon commenting on the reaction of London councillors to the 1848 Public Health Act; the cartoon was published in the humorous magazine,* Punch

# The 1875 Public Health Act

- In 1867, working-class men living in towns were given the vote. Political parties realised that if they promised to improve conditions they would get votes.

- Second Public Health Act, 1875: local councils had to appoint Medical Officers to be responsible for public health; councils were ordered to build sewers, supply fresh water and collect the rubbish.

## SUMMARY

- People moved from the country to towns to find work in the new factories.

- Cities became very overcrowded. Living conditions were terrible, and diseases like typhoid, tuberculosis and cholera were common.

- Many believed that disease was spread by miasma: an 'infectious mist' given off by rotting animals, rubbish and human waste.

- Chadwick's 1842 report highlighted poor conditions in the cities.

- At this time, many thought politicians should not meddle in citizen's lives (laissez-faire).

- The Public Health Act of 1848 set up a Central Board of Health and allowed towns to arrange Local Boards of Health.

- In 1854, Dr Snow realised the link between contaminated water and cholera.

- After the Great Stink, Joseph Bazalgette built a new sewer system for London.

- In 1875 the Second Public Health Act ordered local councils to appoint Medical Officers for health, remove rubbish and sewage, and supply fresh water.

 **APPLY**

### SOURCE ANALYSIS

**a** Write a definition of the following important key words and terms:

- back-to-back housing
- miasma theory
- cholera
- laissez-faire
- Great Stink.

**b** Create a spider diagram about Edwin Chadwick and his work. Use colours and small images to make the information memorable.

**c** Create a timeline containing the key dates about government and public health.

**d** Describe in your own words what is happening in the cartoon in **Source A.**

**e**

> **EXAM QUESTION** Look at **Source A**. How useful is **Source A** to a historian trying to understand the development of public health in the nineteenth century?

### EXAMINER TIP

The source is making reference to a biblical expression, 'cast pearls before swine', meaning to provide something valuable to people who do not recognise its value.

## CHAPTER 10

# Modern treatment of disease

 **RECAP**

## Prevention and cure

During the 1800s, knowledge about disease increased greatly. Doctors and scientists discovered which bacteria caused which diseases. A search began to find ways of **preventing** people from getting the diseases, and also **curing** people who already had these diseases.

**REVIEW**

Look back at pages 38–39 to refresh your memory of the advances made by Pasteur and Koch in understanding infection and bacteria, and the development of the first vaccines.

## Magic bullets

- Robert Koch's assistant, Paul Ehrlich, found chemicals that would not only stain a specific type of bacteria, but kill it too!

- Ehrlich discovered a chemical cure for syphilis in 1909.

- The chemical cures were known as '**magic bullets**'.

- Prontosil, a red chemical, worked against the germs that caused blood poisoning.

- More magic bullets or 'sulpha drugs' were developed to cure or control meningitis, pneumonia and scarlet fever.

## The first antibiotic

By the 1920s, the highly-resistant **Staphylococcus** bacteria (which could cause food and blood poisoning) remained undefeated by any magic bullet

During the First World War, the bacteriologist Alexander Fleming had seen how soldiers were suffering from the ill effects of the Staphylococcus germ

In 1928, Fleming went on holiday and left several plates of Staphylococcus germs on a bench in his laboratory; when he came home, he noticed a large blob of mould in one of the dishes

Fleming became determined to find a better way to treat infected wounds and conducted detailed experiments

Upon investigation, he noticed that the Staphylococcus germs next to the mould had been killed

Fleming took a sample of the mould, and found it to be the penicillin mould; it appeared that a **spore** from this mould, grown in a room below Fleming's, had floated up the stairs and into his laboratory

Alexander Fleming at work in his laboratory

**REVISION SKILLS**

Break down the information for a topic in different ways. You can create a brief fact file containing two or three important points about a person or key people. Try doing this for Alexander Fleming.

Fleming realised the germ-killing capabilities of penicillin and published his findings that year. Even though we know today that penicillin is an **antibiotic**, Fleming did not realise this and concluded that it was a natural antiseptic.

Fleming didn't inject penicillin into an infected animal, which would have shown that it could be used to kill infections. This would likely have sparked great interest in penicillin and could have advanced its development.

As a result, few people regarded Fleming's work as a major breakthrough and gradually even Fleming himself lost interest in it.

**EXAMINER TIP**

This activity can help you plan for an exam question asking you to decide whether a factor such as chance or war is the main factor in a 16-mark question asking about the development of penicillin.

## APPLY

**FACTORS**

**a** Write short definitions for the following key words:

- magic bullet
- Staphylococcus
- antibiotic.

**b** Write brief descriptions of the work of Paul Ehrlich and Alexander Fleming.

**c** In what way was Ehrlich's way of treating illness different from Pasteur's?

**d** Write down an example of how each of the following factors played a part in the discovery of penicillin:

- role of the individual
- science and technology
- chance
- war
- communication.

**REVISION SKILLS**

For longer questions always plan your answer. Aim to write three paragraphs and a conclusion. Jot down a few points to give a shape to your answer. Practise planning answers to questions.

# The development of penicillin

We know today that penicillin is an antibiotic, but Fleming didn't realise this at the time and thought it was a natural antiseptic.

- In the 1930s, researchers at Oxford University read about penicillin's ability to kill germs.

- Scientists Howard Florey and Ernst Chain successfully tested penicillin on eight mice.

- Their next move was to test it on humans and, over a period of months, they produced enough penicillin to use on a patient with a bad infection.

- When the patient was injected with penicillin, the infection began to clear up. However, the patient died when the penicillin ran out. The next step was to try to work out how to produce masses of it.

# How was penicillin mass-produced?

- The Second World War was a major factor in transforming the supply of penicillin because a steady supply of it was vital in treating soldiers with infected wounds.

- In June 1941, Florey met with the US government who agreed to pay several huge chemical companies to make millions of gallons of it.

- By the end of the war in 1945, Britain and the USA were working closely together and 250,000 soldiers were being treated. Drug companies began using their production methods to make penicillin for public use as soon as the war ended.

▼ **SOURCE A** *Penicillin being mass-produced in the 1940s; a worker at Pfizer is shown carefully preparing vials of penicillin solution*

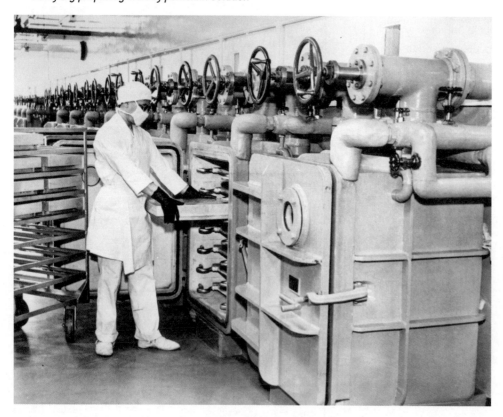

# The development of the pharmaceutical industry

| | | |
|---|---|---|
| Towards the end of the nineteenth century, some of the larger companies we know today (GlaxoSmithKline, Beecham, Hoffmann-La Roche and Pfizer) had been formed: they started out as chemists and pill-makers, or producers of chemicals used by scientists | The discovery of penicillin led to huge government-sponsored programmes to develop and produce it; this meant that the pharmaceutical industry had both the finance and the technology to research and develop medicines for all sorts of diseases | Today, the pharmaceutical industry is one of the biggest in the world, worth an estimated £200 billion to £300 billion and employing nearly 80,000 people in the UK alone. |

## The impact of penicillin

- Around 15 per cent of wounded British and US soldiers would have died without penicillin.
- Thousands of injured soldiers returned to service much more quickly than they would have done without penicillin treatment.
- After the war, penicillin became available for doctors. It was classified as an antibiotic, and has gone on to save the lives of millions of people.
- Other antibiotics followed: streptomycin (1944), for example, proved an excellent treatment for tuberculosis, while tetracycline (1953) was great for clearing up skin infections. Mitomycin (1956) has been used as a chemotherapy drug for treating several different types of cancer.

 **APPLY**

### FACTORS

a   Briefly describe the work of Florey and Chain in the development of penicillin.

b   Look back at the notes you made about factors relating to the discovery of penicillin in the activity on page 45. To remind you, the factors were: role of the individual; science and technology; chance; war; communication. Based on the work you have done on these pages, can you add any more notes or examples relating to the development of penicillin?

c   You are required to think about seven factors in total. Five are listed above; the other two are **government** and **religion**. Can you write down any examples of these two factors for the development of penicillin?

d   **EXAM QUESTION** Was war the main factor in the development of penicillin? Explain your answer with reference to war and other factors.

**EXAMINER TIP**

Refer to two other factors such as government and the role of the individual in order to targe ... grades.

# Science and treatment into the twenty-first century

The second half of the twentieth century saw an explosion in scientific and medical discoveries and developments that proved significant in achieving a fuller understanding of health and medicine.

The diagram below shows some of the most significant changes in the fields of knowledge about the body and disease, surgery, and treatment:

### Body and disease

1953: stem cells (multi-cellular organisms that are able to renew themselves) discovered; in 2013, the first human liver was grown from stem cells

1953: scientists at Cambridge University (Francis Crick and James Watson) map out the DNA structure; the understanding of DNA leads to such developments as gene therapy, genetic screening and genetic engineering

1970s and 1980s: technology that we take for granted today was developed: CAT scanners that produce 3D images of the body (1973); endoscope probes that allow doctors to 'see' inside the body (1975); MRI scanning (1987)

### Key developments in health and medicine since 1945

### Treatment

Between 1946 and 1969: free vaccines available in the UK for TB, diphtheria, whooping cough, tetanus, polio, measles and rubella (German measles)

1957: the drug thalidomide is developed in Germany; used to treat morning sickness during pregnancy but causes terrible deformities in babies

1970: a British scientist develops the drug cyclosporine, which prevents the body rejecting transplanted organs

1978: doctors use IVF fertility treatment to help childless women become pregnant

### Surgery

1950: first open-heart surgery to repair a 'hole' in a baby's heart; first pacemaker is fitted in 1958, followed by the first British heart transplant (1968)

Livers, lungs, kidneys, pancreases, bone marrow (and even faces) can also be transplanted today

Miniature hearing aids (1952), hip replacements (1972) and skin grafts (1984) are now common

# Factors in twentieth-century medical developments

## Technology

- New technologies such as keyhole surgery and MRI scanning help doctors and surgeons develop new techniques for identifying illnesses and operating on them.

- Discoveries, such as understanding more about DNA, have helped gene researchers find specific genes involved in diseases.

## War

- Two world wars meant that the government spent a fortune on research, and testing drugs and surgical techniques.

- Doctors had to find better ways to treat casualties too.

## Change in attitudes

- Modern politicians have realised that one of their main priorities is to help and protect the people they serve. 'Healthy Eating Standards' in schools is a good example of this.

## Government and finance

- Governments spend far more money on research and care than ever before.

- Drug companies spend huge amounts on research and development, hoping to make money from cures.

## Communication

- New ideas spread rapidly due to the increased use of television, news media and the Internet.

- Television and radio advertisements have made more people than ever before aware of health risks.

## Individual character

- As across all periods of history, the late twentieth century saw some geniuses in action: Crick and Watson mapping DNA structure, for example.

# Antibiotic resistance

- The effectiveness of antibiotics can lead to their overuse, prompting bacteria to evolve and become increasingly resistant to common antibiotics.

- An example of an antibiotics-resistant bacteria is called MRSA (methicillin-resistant Staphylococcus aureus), first reported in a British study in 1961.

# Alternative treatments and 'positive health'

- Since the 1980s, alternative therapies have become more and more popular in Britain, and some of them (such as acupuncture, hypnotherapy and aromatherapy) are now available on the NHS.

- In recent years, there has been a greater emphasis placed on prevention rather than cure – this is

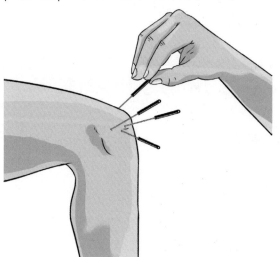

sometimes known as 'positive health'. People are learning that regular exercise and a good diet can help prevent killers such as obesity and heart disease.

- There has also been an increase in screening, which focuses on checking people who seem to be healthy, aiming to find those who have the early signs of a serious illness like lung or breast cancer.

## SUMMARY

- The discovery and development of the first antibiotic (penicillin) by Fleming, Florey and Chain was a significant moment in medical history.

- A number of factors combined in the development and discovery of penicillin.

- The second half of the twentieth century saw many scientific and medical discoveries and developments that proved significant in achieving a fuller understanding of health and medicine.

- Overuse of antibiotics can prompt bacteria to evolve and become increasingly resistant.

- In recent years, alternative therapies such as acupuncture, hypnotherapy and aromatherapy have become more and more popular in Britain.

## ⚙ APPLY

### EXPLAIN THE SIGNIFICANCE

**a** Write a short sentence (no more than 15 words) to explain each of the following terms:

- antibiotic resistance
- alternative therapies.

**b** Give two examples of each of the following:

- developments in treatments since the Second World War
- developments in surgery since the Second World War
- developments in understanding the body and disease since the Second World War.

**c** Suggest reasons why drugs and treatments have developed greatly in the late twentieth century.

**d** | EXAM QUESTION | Explain the significance of antibiotic resistance in the development of medicine.

# CHAPTER 11

# The impact of war and technology on surgery

## Wartime developments: plastic surgery, blood transfusions and X-rays

Some types of medicine develop at a greater rate during wartime than in peacetime.

- Governments spend a lot of money on the development of the latest medical techniques and the most up-to-date medical technology.

- They know that if medical services are good, then more soldiers have a chance of survival; and the more soldiers there are available, the greater the country's chances of victory.

- Doctors and surgeons work very hard in wartime, often in battlefield situations, to develop their ideas in order to treat the injured.

- The huge numbers of wounded soldiers give doctors and surgeons more opportunities than are available in peacetime to test their ideas out.

### X-rays

Discovered in 1895; hospitals used them to look for broken bones and disease before the First World War

During the war, proved their effectiveness on the battlefield when mobile X-ray machines were used, developed by Polish scientist Marie Curie

Allowed surgeons to find out exactly where in the wounded soldier's body bullets or pieces of shrapnel had lodged – without having to cut him open

### The impact of the First and Second World Wars

### Plastic surgery

During the First World War, Harold Gillies (a London-based army doctor) set up a special unit to graft (transplant) skin and treat men suffering from severe facial wounds

Queen's Hospital in Kent opened in 1917; by 1921 it provided over 1000 beds for soldiers with severe facial wounds

During the Second World War, Archibald McIndoe used new drugs such as penicillin to prevent infection when treating pilots with horrific facial injuries

### Blood transfusions

In 1900, Karl Landsteiner discovered blood groups, which helped doctors work out that a transfusion only worked if the donor's blood type matched the receiver's

It was not possible to store blood for long until 1914 when Albert Hustin discovered that sodium citrate stopped blood from clotting

British National Blood Transfusion Service opened in 1938

Large blood banks developed in both the USA and Britain during the Second World War

## Other developments relating to the wars

**Broken bones**: new techniques were developed during the First World War to repair broken bones. For example, the Army Leg Splint (or Keller-Blake Splint) was developed, which kept a broken leg 'in traction'. The splint is still in use today.

**Heart surgery**: this progressed during the Second World War. US army surgeon Dwight Harken, stationed in London, cut into beating hearts and used his bare hands to remove bullets and bits of shrapnel.

**Diet**: as a result of food shortages during wartime, many people grew their own food. This improved their diets because the food the government encouraged people to grow – fresh vegetables for example – was very healthy.

**Hygiene and disease**: in order to keep Britain 'fighting fit' during the Second World War, there was a campaign that warned against the dangers of poor hygiene. A national immunisation programme against diphtheria (a bacterial infection which killed many children) was launched during the war too.

**Drug development**: penicillin, the first antibiotic, was developed in the years leading up to the Second World War. The British and US governments realised how important this new 'wonder drug' could be in curing infections in deep wounds. By 1944, enough penicillin was produced to treat all the Allied forces in Europe.

# Negative effects on medical progress

Some historians argue that war can sometimes have a negative effect on medical progress too.

- Thousands of doctors are taken away from their normal work to treat casualties.

- Some medical research is stopped during wartime so countries can concentrate everything on the war effort.

- Throughout history, warfare has disrupted towns and cities, sometimes destroying libraries and places of learning. Medical advances may have been delayed because these places were destroyed and manuscripts and research lost.

 **APPLY**

**FACTORS**

a Explain why medicine can often develop at a greater rate during wartime than in peacetime.

b Describe the role played by each of the following people in the development of medicine during the world wars:

- Marie Curie

- Harold Gillies

- Archibald McIndoe

- Albert Hustin.

c Identify a way in which warfare has helped:

- public health

- in the fight against infection.

 **EXAMINER TIP**

This activity will help you to plan for a factors question that asks you to consider war as a factor.

**REVISION SKILLS**

Use sketches, doodles and pictures to help make facts memorable. You do not have to be a good artist to do this!

# Modern surgical methods

Major technological breakthroughs continued in the field of surgery after the world wars. Improved anaesthetics allowed patients to be unconscious for longer, so more complicated operations could be attempted, while better antiseptics increased the success rate of difficult operations because they cut down the chances of deadly infection. Scientific and technological advances have led to dramatic changes in the way doctors can treat some medical conditions.

# Transplant surgery

## Timeline

**▼ 1952**

■ The first transplant of a whole organ (a kidney) is carried out; the first in the UK is in 1960

**▼ 1967**

■ Christian Barnard, a South African heart surgeon, performs the first heart transplant; the patient lives for 18 days (the first in the UK is in 1968)

**▼ 1970**

■ British scientist Roy Calne develops the drug cyclosporine, which prevents the body rejecting transplanted organs

**▼ 1986**

■ British woman Davina Thompson becomes the first heart, lung and liver transplant patient

**▼ 2006**

■ First partial face transplant is carried out

**▼ 2008**

■ First full face transplant

# Other modern surgical methods

**Keyhole surgery**: surgeons can now perform operations through very small cuts. Using miniaturised instruments and small fibre-optic cameras linked to computers, surgeons can magnify the areas they are working on so they can re-join nerves and blood vessels.

**Radiation therapy** (also known as radiotherapy): although this has been used for over 100 years, the methods of treatment are developing all the time. Radiation therapy involves the use of high-energy radiation to shrink tumours and kill cancer cells. Sometimes a radioactive substance such as radioactive iodine is used, which travels in the blood to kill cancer cells.

**Laser surgery**: surgery using lasers (rather than a scalpel) has become increasingly popular since a laser was first used in an eye operation in 1987. Lasers are increasingly used to treat a variety of skin conditions, help clear blocked arteries, remove tumours and ulcers, and control bleeding.

## SUMMARY

- Some types of medicine can develop at a greater rate during wartime than in peacetime.

- During wartime, governments spend lots of money on the development of the latest medical techniques. They know that if medical services are good, then more injured soldiers will get fitter quicker and back on the battlefield.

- The First World War saw major developments in the fields of X-rays, blood transfusions and plastic surgery.

- The Second World War saw major developments in plastic surgery and drug treatments.

- Scientific and technological advances have led to dramatic changes in the way doctors have treated some medical conditions since the war.

- Some of the latest surgical methods include laser surgery, keyhole surgery and radiation therapy.

 **APPLY**

**SOURCE ANALYSIS**

◄ **SOURCE A** *A poster from 1943, produced by the Ministry of Information; it shows the official Army Blood Transfusion appointment card and has space at the bottom for local centres to provide information on dates and times when people can attend to give blood*

**a** Write a short definition (no more than 15 words) for:

- keyhole surgery
- laser surgery
- radiation therapy.

**b** Look back through pages 44–53 and try to find examples of how medical progress has been affected by:

- war
- superstition and religion
- chance
- government
- communication
- science and technology
- the role of the individual in encouraging or inhibiting change.

**c**

 Study **Source A**. How useful is **Source A** to a historian studying the relationship between war and medicine?

**REVISION SKILLS**

Create a 10-point fact test to test detailed knowledge about a topic. You can swap the test with a friend.

# Modern public health

## Britain in 1900 and after

- By 1900, millions of ordinary British citizens were still living in desperate poverty.

- Overcrowded, unsanitary housing was still common in Britain's industrial towns.

- People worked long hours for low wages and could not afford decent food or to see a doctor if they were ill.

- After 1900, the government began to have more involvement in public health.

## The reports of Booth and Rowntree

At the beginning of the twentieth century, two special investigations highlighted the plight of the poor.

### Charles Booth's report

Called *Life and Labour of the People in London*

Found that around 30 per cent of Londoners were so poor that they didn't have enough money to eat properly, despite having full-time jobs

Demonstrated that there was a link between poverty and a high death rate

### Seebohm Rowntree's report

Called *Poverty: A Study of Town Life*; his investigations took place in York

Found that 28 per cent of the population did not have the minimum amount of money to live on at some time of their life

## The Boer War

- In 1899, a large-scale army recruitment campaign took place to find men to fight in the Boer War.

- Army chiefs were alarmed by the fact that 40 per cent of the young men who volunteered were unfit to be soldiers, mostly due to poor diet and poverty-related illnesses.

- The government set up a special committee to enquire into the 'Physical Deterioration of the People'.

- In 1904, the committee released its report, concluding that many men were failing to get into the army because they led such unhealthy lives.

## Government action on public health

- The reports fuelled fears that the unhealthy state of Britain's workers might lead to the decline of Britain as a great industrial power. Germany, for example, which had a good system of state welfare for workers, was beginning to produce as much coal, iron and steel as Britain.

- Some politicians, including many from the Liberal Party (including Winston Churchill and David Lloyd George), believed that direct action from the government was the way to improve the public health, welfare and productivity of the nation.

- The Liberal Party was also worried about the popularity of the Labour Party, which had been founded in 1900, so they wanted measures that would appeal to working people and stop them voting for Labour.

## The Liberal reforms

In 1906, the Liberal Party won the general election and took action.

Timeline:

### ▼ 1906

- Free school meals provided for poor children

### ▼ 1907

- School medical service set up – free medical inspections, followed later by free treatment

### ▼ 1908

- Children and Young Person's Act introduced; children become 'protected persons', which means that parents are breaking the law if they neglect their children

## 1908

Old Age Pensions are introduced, paid for by national taxes

## 1909

Britain's first job centres are built

## 1911

National Insurance Act introduces unemployment benefit ('the dole'), free medical treatment, and sickness pay

## APPLY

### SOURCE ANALYSIS

**a** Suggest reasons why the government became more concerned about public health in the early years of the twentieth century.

**b** Make five revision cards on the Liberal reforms, using these titles for each card: Who were the Liberals?; Why did the Liberals make reforms?; Reforms aimed at children; Reforms aimed at the elderly; Reforms aimed at the sick and unemployed.

**c**  **EXAM QUESTION** Study **Source A**. How useful is **Source A** to a historian studying the impact of the Liberal reforms?

▼ **SOURCE A** *This chart from 1907 shows the impact of free school meals; it charts the weight children gained (and lost) during part of the school year*

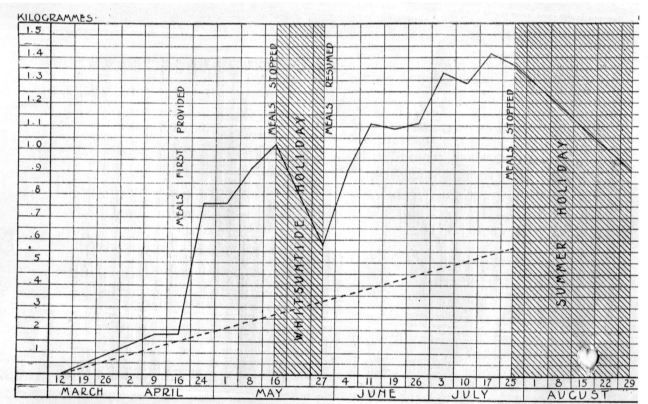

CHART ILLUSTRATING THE AVERAGE GAIN OR LOSS IN WEIGHT - DURING THE INTERVALS SHEWN OF THE CHILDREN WHO WERE FED. THE BROKEN LINE SHEWS THE AVERAGE INCREASE IN WEIGHT DURING THE SAME TIME - OF THE CONTROL CHILDREN.

### REVISION SKILLS

Repetition is vital for good long-term memory. Plan revision sessions in short bursts of 20 to 30 minutes several times a day.

# The welfare state

During the Second World War, the Beveridge Report argued that the state should provide support for vulnerable people. This led to the creation of the 'welfare state'.

# Impact of two world wars on public health

- The need for healthy soldiers to defend Britain highlighted the importance of tackling poverty and poor health.
- After the First World War, the building of overcrowded back-to-back housing was banned.
- In 1918, local councils had to provide health visitors, clinics for pregnant women, and day nurseries.
- In 1919, councils began to build new houses for poorer families and, by 1930, a huge slum clearance programme had started.
- But during the Second World War people were shocked at the health of the evacuated city children.

## The Beveridge Report

In 1942, a report about the state of Britain by Sir William Beveridge (an economist and social reformer) sold over 100,000 copies in its first month of publication.

It said that people had a right to be free of the 'five giants' that could ruin their lives:

- disease
- want (need)
- ignorance
- idleness
- squalor (very poor living conditions).

The report suggested ways to improve quality of life, and said that the government should 'take charge of social security from the cradle to the grave'.

# The Labour government and the welfare state

After the war the Labour Party, led by Clement Attlee, won the election by promising to follow Beveridge's advice and set up the welfare state to look after the sick, the unemployed and children.

## The welfare state

The National Health Service (NHS) began in 1948 to provide free health treatment for everyone.

A weekly family allowance payment helped with childcare costs.

The very poor received financial help or 'benefits'.

More slums were demolished and new houses built. Twelve new towns were created. By 1948, 280,000 council homes were being built each year.

# Development of the NHS

- When Aneurin Bevan (Labour Minister for Health) introduced the NHS in 1948 he overcame opposition from doctors who did not wish to come under government control or lose income.
- Bevan won them over by promising them a salary and allowing them to treat private patients as well.
- Over the years, the cost of welfare state services like the NHS has rocketed. In 2015–16 the NHS budget was £116 billion in total.
- The NHS is not totally free. Working people today have to pay for doctors' prescriptions and dental treatment.

## REVISION SKILLS

Write facts on notes and stick them up together in a specific part of your room or house. When you go or look there you will read your notes and associate that part of the room or house with that topic.

## Healthcare in the twenty-first century

- Modern drugs are very expensive and modern medicine means that people are living longer – so there are more elderly people than ever before. Older people tend to use the services of the NHS more than younger people.

- Healthy eating campaigns and new laws try to protect Britain's citizens and prevent them from needing expensive medical care in the future. Tobacco advertising, for example, was banned in 2005.

- Initiatives such as checking for the early signs of cancer, understanding how to spot (and deal with) a potential stroke victim, and trying to encourage people to eat five portions of fruit and vegetables a day are all aimed at making Britain healthier.

- Technological breakthroughs and developments will also continue to improve the health and wellbeing of people. 'Digital therapy', for example, is designed for patients who need at-home care or who can't travel to a doctor's surgery or hospital.

### SUMMARY

- After 1900, the government began to have more involvement in public health.

- In 1906, the Liberal government introduced a series of reforms aimed at helping Britain's most vulnerable people.

- The Beveridge Report (1942) led to the creation of the welfare state and the NHS.

- At first, doctors opposed the creation of the NHS.

- Today, the NHS faces many challenges – modern medicine is expensive so costs are spiralling, and people are living longer and elderly people are more likely to require a greater amount of NHS time and resources.

  **APPLY**

### SIMILARITY

**a** List ways in which the British government tried to improve public health in the twentieth century.

**b** Write a sentence about the role of each of the following in improving Britain's health in the twentieth century:

- Charles Booth
- Seebohm Rowntree
- Sir William Beveridge
- Clement Atlee
- Aneurin Bevan.

**c** Construct a spider diagram about the NHS. There should be branches that cover: When (did it begin)? Why (was it introduced)? How (is it paid for)? Who (are the key figures involved)? What (services does it provide) and (are some of the problems associated with it)?

**d**

> EXAM QUESTION
>
> Explain two ways in which the reasons for improvements in public health in the nineteenth century and the reasons for improvements in public health in the twentieth century were similar.

**REVIEW**

Look back at Chapter 9 to refresh your memory of the reasons for improvements in public health in the nineteenth century.

**EXAMINER TIP**

Make sure you know the question types you will be asked in each part of the examination. Find out how many marks there are for each type of question.

## GCSE sample answers

### ⟳ REVIEW

On these exam practice pages, you will find a sample student answer for each of the exam questions for Paper 2 Britain: Health and the People Thematic Study. What are the strengths and weaknesses of the answers? Read the following pages and think carefully about what the student has written, what the examiner has said about each answer, and how you might improve your own answers to the Health and the People exam questions.

### The source analysis question

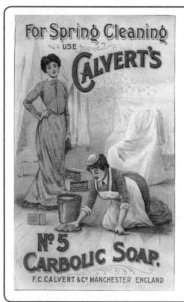

 **SOURCE A** *An advertisement for soap, published in a women's magazine in 1910. Professor Frederick Crace-Calvert was a chemist who studied in Paris before returning to Manchester where he set up a company in 1859. He discovered the way to make large quantities of carbolic acid; his company sent supplies to Joseph Lister*

**EXAM QUESTION** **1** Study **Source A**. How useful is **Source A** to a historian studying the understanding of disease? Explain your answer by using **Source A** and your contextual knowledge.

**8 marks**

### Sample student answer

The advert shows a servant scrubbing the floor with carbolic soap while a woman watches. People now realised that germs caused disease because Joseph Lister made Pasteur's ideas understood in Britain. Lister used carbolic acid to kill germs in surgery, and battled to get his antiseptic methods accepted from the 1870s. Lister was opposed by surgeons who had their own ways of cleaning wounds, disliked the fuss of carbolic, or simply disagreed that germs were responsible for infection. Some of them, led by Charlton Bastian, believed germs came about by spontaneous generation. Epidemic diseases like cholera were common in nineteenth-century industrial towns. Many people were involved in the debate about the cause and how to stop the epidemics. It was the cattle plague of 1866 that proved decisive and showed that a specific microbe was responsible. This advert is from 1910, much later, and proves that by this time ordinary people realised that not being clean could make you ill and you needed to wash. The anti-contagionist and contagionist views had come together. A historian studying the causes of disease will find a use for this advert as evidence that progress in medical science had an impact on everyday life and that the debate about the role of germs in infection was over.

**EXAMINER TIP**

Try not to write only about what you can see in the picture but also about what facts you know — for example, make sure you go on to write about carbolic acid and the antiseptic method.

**EXAMINER TIP**

The question asks about 'how useful' the source is, and this answer directly refers to the use of the source for the historian's particular interest. In this case the historian is interested in the understanding of disease, and this answer did well to address it.

## OVERALL COMMENT

The answer is a good answer at Level 3 because it uses what can be seen in the picture and adds some extra knowledge. It also uses the provenance of the source in the answer.

## OVER TO YOU

1 Review the sample answer:

  **a** highlight where the answer adds some factual knowledge

  **b** highlight where the answer uses the provenance (caption information).

2 **a** Now have a go at writing your own answer. Remember, in the exam it is recommended that you spend no more than 10 minutes on this question.

  **b** Once you have written your answer, check it against the questions below. Did you…

  ☐ include some detailed facts and figures?

  ☐ remember to refer to the provenance of the source?

  ☐ make your answer relevant to what the historian is studying?

You may find it helpful to look back at Chapters 7–8 to refresh your knowledge of Germ Theory and its impact on the treatment of disease.

## The 'significance' question

 **2** Explain the significance of Paré's work for the development of medicine.

8 marks

### Sample student answer

Paré was significant because he questioned the traditional way of dealing with gunshot wounds. He found out by accident that cauterising was not necessary and that the soothing cream helped wounds heal better. Paré also revived Galen's use of ligatures to tie off and stop bleeding. Although ligatures were less painful, they might introduce infection and slowed amputations on the battlefield. All this means that Paré observed, experimented and questioned the way he was treating his patients. It was significant that his discoveries spread throughout Europe.

## OVERALL COMMENT

The answer is one that should reach Level 3. However the second point about the spread of his discoveries is not developed. It would be good if the answer referred to the popularity of Paré's book, the many translations and editions of it, and the treatments it contained.

**REVISION SKILLS**

Remind yourself about provenance. Look back to 'how to master the source question' on pages 7–8.

**EXAMINER TIP**

Lister was a surgeon, so it is important to say how this advert fits into the debate about public health in the late nineteenth century. Try to name people who were influential in the debate about disease. Mention events that might be seen as the turning points in the greater public understanding of disease in the late nineteenth century.

**EXAMINER TIP**

The answer shows knowledge of what Paré did and explains it using the correct technical terms.

**EXAMINER TIP**

The answer identifies more than one significance. The first significance about Paré's methods is explained well, but the second about the spread of his discoveries is not developed enough.

## OVER TO YOU

**1** Review the sample answer:

   **a** highlight the technical terms used in the answer

   **b** highlight where the answer mentions Paré's approach or methods.

**2 a** Now have a go at writing your own answer. Remember, in the exam it is recommended that you spend no more than 10 minutes on this question.

   **b** Once you have written your answer, check it against the questions below. Did you…

   ☐ include some detailed knowledge?

   ☐ remember to provide at least two examples of the significance of Paré and his work?

You may find it helpful to look back at Chapter 4 to refresh your knowledge of Paré and the Renaissance.

**EXAMINER TIP**

You should explain how Paré's discoveries spread throughout Europe. Try to say how Paré's work was made popular in England. It is also important to appreciate how Paré's work showed the impact of the Renaissance.

## The 'similarity' question

**EXAM QUESTION**

**3** Explain two ways in which medieval hospitals and eighteenth-century hospitals were similar.

8 marks

### Sample student answer

They are similar because rich people liked to set up hospitals in both the Middle Ages and the eighteenth century. Kings and noblemen gave money to set up hospitals such as St Leonard's, paid for by the Norman King Stephen. However these hospitals were often small, having only 12 places – as many as Christ had disciples. Patrons of hospitals followed Christ's example of healing the sick. In the eighteenth century wealthy people like the merchant, Thomas Guy, set up hospitals – such as Guy's Hospital in 1724. In both Islamic hospitals and the eighteenth century ones, doctors tried to use a scientific approach. John Hunter was a surgeon at a hospital in London. He taught Edward Jenner anatomy and surgery.

**EXAMINER TIP**

This answer is good because it immediately identifies a similarity.

**EXAMINER TIP**

The student has done well to include factual knowledge from both periods in support of the similarity identified.

**EXAMINER TIP**

The answer makes a valid but weak additional point about some doctors using a scientific approach in both periods. However the answer does not give any evidence to support that similarity.

### OVERALL COMMENT

This answer is a low Level 3. It shows some detailed knowledge but more needs to be added about the scientific approach adopted by Islamic doctors and the surgeon John Hunter.

**OVER TO YOU**

1 Review the sample answer:

  **a** highlight where the answer shows it is concerned with similarity

  **b** highlight where the answer shows relevant knowledge

  **c** highlight where the answer adds knowledge that is not directly related to the question.

2 **a** Now have a go at writing your own answer. Remember, in the exam it is recommended that you spend no more than 10 minutes on this question.

  **b** Once you have written your answer, check it against the questions below. Did you…

  ☐ suggest at least two similarities?

  ☐ make sure that they share a common theme or point?

  ☐ include some detailed facts from your own knowledge to support each similarity?

You may find it helpful to look back at Chapters 1, 2 and 5 to refresh your knowledge of the Middle Ages and the eighteenth century.

**EXAMINER TIP**

Include in your answer some extra knowledge about Medieval, Islamic, and eighteenth-century hospitals that would support the final point that doctors at both times approached medicine in a scientific way.

## The 'main factors' question

**EXAM QUESTION**

4 Has government been the main factor that has led to improvements in public health? Explain your answer with reference to government and other factors.

**16 marks**  **SPaG 4 marks**

### Sample student answer

Government has always been an important factor in improving public health. Local government in Medieval towns tried to stop bad smells and people polluting the environment. In 1371, councillors in London passed a law to ban butchers killing large animals within the city walls. But the authorities in Medieval times needed the money and the motivation to pay for improved sanitation. Towns were wealthy through trade but councillors risked unpopularity if they forced people to pay taxes to clean up areas, and they did not know about germs.

In the early nineteenth century government was reluctant to improve public health because it followed the idea of laissez-faire – not interfering in how people lived their lives. However, epidemics like cholera, which came to Britain in 1831 and killed 50,000 people, made the government take action. They passed a Public Health Act (1848) which gave local authorities powers to clean up their areas. Government in Britain made it compulsory for local authorities to improve public health in 1875. Another Public Health Act was needed when it was proved that cholera was passed on through contaminated water. Governments have the power and wealth which allows them to improve the health of everyone such as by introducing the National Health Service which began in 1948.

**EXAMINER TIP**

This answer is good because it uses examples of the actions of government in different periods – the Middle Ages, and the nineteenth and twentieth centuries.

**EXAMINER TIP**

The answer will gain marks because it has plenty of factual knowledge to support its understanding.

There have been other factors that have improved public health such as the scientific understanding of disease. As science developed so people understood the causes of disease better. Epidemics like the Black Death in 1348 were explained by people in the Middle Ages as a punishment from God for their sins. In the Middle Ages people did not know about germs. There were no microscopes powerful enough to see the germs, but as technology improved scientists noticed germs. However they did not fully understand how they caused disease until Pasteur's work in the nineteenth century. People thought that disease could be transmitted through the air by poisons or a miasma. In the 1860s Pasteur showed that germs cause disease. Robert Koch identified specific germs that caused tuberculosis (1882) and cholera (1883). Science showed why it was important to improve public health by providing a clean environment.

**EXAMINER TIP**

This answer explains how another factor – science and technology – has led to improvements in public health.

## OVERALL COMMENT

The answer is good because it uses examples of leadership and government from across the whole time period covered by the unit, 'Health and the People'. It is likely to receive a Level 3 mark because it has discussed government as well as another factor that has improved public health. There is good spelling and grammar in the answer and it uses the correct historical terms. However to be sure of a Level 3 mark it would benefit from another factor, and then a conclusion that evaluates the impact of these factors and assesses whether 'government' was indeed the 'main' factor in improving public health.

## OVER TO YOU

1   Review the sample answer. Highlight where the following are mentioned:

   **a**   specific diseases

   **b**   theories about the cause of disease

   **c**   laws and rules

   **d**   how each factor acted to improve public health.

2   Now have a go at writing your own answer. Remember, in the exam it is recommended that you spend no more than 20 minutes on this question.

   **a**   Write a paragraph about another factor involved in improving public health, such as knowledge about warfare, individuals, technology or religion.

   **b**   Write a conclusion in which you decide which was the *main* factor.

   **c**   Once you have written your answer, check it against the questions below. Did you…

   ☐   write about a factor other than the one mentioned in the question?

   ☐   add some factual knowledge of your own?

   ☐   make a decision about which factor was the main factor?

   ☐   check your answer for correct spellings, punctuation and grammar?

**EXAMINER TIP**

You only have 20 minutes to answer this question so a paragraph should take about 5 minutes. Think about including a reference to each of the aspects (a-d) above and how they relate to the factor that you have chosen to write about.

The answers provided here are examples, based on the information provided in the RECAP sections of this Revision Guide. There may be other factors which are relevant to each question, and you should draw on as much own knowledge as possible to give detailed and precise answers. There are also many ways of answering exam questions (for example, of structuring an essay). However, these exemplar answers should provide a good starting point.

## Chapter 1
### Page 13
**SOURCE ANALYSIS**

**a** Choose two from: the presence of nuns, a priest giving sacraments to a dying patient, an altar with a crucifix above it.

**b** The source is useful because it shows:
- the control of the Catholic Church in late Medieval Europe
- the belief that God might cause illness
- that Christians should help the sick – on the right the sick are comforted
- the king praying in the picture – his doctors worked in the hospital
- that hospitals were small – they often had only 12 patients
- people dying and receiving the last rites, and bodies being bound for burial.

**FACTORS**

**Christianity helped medical progress and treatments:**
- The Christian Church believed in following the example of Jesus who healed the sick; therefore Christians believed it was good to look after the sick.
- Monks preserved and copied by hand ancient medical texts.
- Christians believed in caring for the sick and started many hospitals; over 700 set up in England between 1000 and 1500.
- Hospitals were funded by charity or a wealthy patron, for example St Leonard's hospital was paid for by the Norman King Stephen.
- Hospitals concentrated on caring for the sick, not curing, and many had a priest rather than a doctor.

**Christianity hindered medical progress and treatments:**
- People believed God sent illness as a punishment (e.g. mental illness) or a test of faith; curing an illness might be seen as a challenge to God's will.
- Prayers were seen as the most important treatments, not drugs.
- The Church believed in miraculous healing and the sick were encouraged to visit shrines (a pilgrimage) containing the relics of a holy person, and pray to saints to cure their illness.
- The Church arrested the thirteenth century English monk, Roger Bacon, for suggesting doctors should do original research and not trust old books.
- The Church approved the medical ideas of the ancient Greeks and Romans; these were taught in universities.

## Chapter 2
### Page 15
**SIGNIFICANCE**

**c** **Knowledge**:
- Islam encouraged medical learning and discoveries
- Islam preserved medical texts from the ancient world

**Treatments:**
- scientists discovered new drugs like senna
- Islam treated mental illness sympathetically

**d** It was part of the Islamic faith to search for cures and scientific discoveries. Also, the Caliph's government of the Islamic empire approved of and encouraged medical discoveries.

**e** The knowledge of the ancient world returned to Western Europe in books brought by scholars in the eleventh century. The universities in Italy taught the medical ideas of the ancient world and those discovered and incorporated by Islamic doctors through trade – merchants shipped books, drugs, and people with knowledge of Islamic medicine to Western Europe

**f** Answers might include reference to:
- preserving the knowledge of the ancient world during the Early Middle Ages in Western Europe
- adding to the store of medical knowledge
- following a scientific approach to medical developments
- discovering new medicines to treat illness.

**FACTORS**

**Government**: Caliph's approved of medical progress, created libraries and endowed hospitals

**Role of the individual**: The eleventh century scholar, Avicenna, wrote a book with over one million words, *Canon of Medicine*, which became the standard medical text

**Communication**: Rhazes wrote over 150 books, Avicenna wrote *Canon of Medicine*; Constantine the African translated many Arabic books into Latin in 1065

**Science and technology**: Muslim scientists discovered new drugs like senna and naphtha; Avicenna wrote about over 760 different drugs; doctors like Ibn al-Nafis believed the blood circulated and Galen was wrong – but there was no dissection allowed!

### Page 17
**SOURCE ANALYSIS**

**a** Bloodletting

**b** Cauterisation

**c** **Name**: Abulcasis
**Location**: Islamic Empire
**Time**: 1000
**Book**: *Al Tasrif*
**Ideas**: New instruments and procedures e.g. cauterisation, ligatures
**Name**: Hugh of Lucca and Theodoric
**Location**: Bologna, Italy
**Time**: 1267
**Book**: Written in 1267
**Ideas**: Wine on wounds, pus not needed for healing to occur, critics of Hippocratic ideas
**Name**: Mondino de Luzzi
**Location**: Bologna, Italy
**Time**: 1316
**Book**: *Anathomia*
**Ideas**: Dissection manual
**Name**: Guy De Chauliac
**Location**: France
**Time**: 1363
**Book**: *Great Surgery*
**Ideas**: Critic of Theodoric of Lucca's ideas; book refers to Greek and Islamic writers like Avicenna
**Name**: John of Arderne
**Location**: London, England
**Time**: 1376
**Book**: *Practica*
**Ideas**: Opium and henbane to dull pain; anal abscess operations; formed Guild of Surgeons

**d** The source might be useful because it:
- shows the importance of monasteries in preserving knowledge
- is an illustration from the fourteenth century showing trepanning
- shows a remedy for headaches/epilepsy/possession by evil spirit
- provides no evidence of anaesthetic or antiseptic.

## Chapter 3
### Page 19
**FACTORS**

**a** Rivers provided water supply for transport, drinking, washing, businesses and removal of waste products e.g. sewage and rubbish.

**b** You should produce your own set of revision cards for this activity.

**c** From local wells

**d** Emptied it into the river, used urine in for wool cleaning, used manure for fertiliser on fields

**e** As well as showing a knowledge of Medieval government and leadership of towns, answers might refer to:
- the wealth of towns
- the knowledge about hygiene at the time.

## Page 21

**a** Stars; bad air; Jewish poisoning, a punishment from God

**b** People did not know the real cause; there were two types of disease with different methods of spreading; public health measures had little impact; SQUALID conditions; crowded towns

**c** Socially whole villages became deserted. The disease killed many people, priests died, and beliefs were challenged. The disease never really went away, with further outbreaks in subsequent centuries. Economically it made manual labour more in demand, therefore there were higher wages and prices for food rose. Longer-term it led to the weakening of the feudal system and the Peasants' Revolt of 1381.

## Chapter 4
## Page 23

**a** People questioned accepted truths, searched for evidence, and experimented with new ideas.

**b** New aspects of the Renaissance included: books/printing, art, inventions, science and learning.

**c** **Before Vesalius**:

Textbooks: followed Galen, never challenged, focused on individual organs

Dissection: used to prove Galen right

Anatomical knowledge: some was based upon Galen's mistakes and animal dissections

**After Vesalius**:

Textbooks: accurate, illustrated, based on dissection, looked at systems within the body e.g. digestions

Dissection: used to find out knowledge

Anatomical knowledge: all based on human anatomy e.g. breastbone shown to be in three parts, not seven as in an ape

**d** • Went against centuries of belief in Galen's work

• Showed a new way of finding out and teaching about anatomy

• Produced an accurate textbook of human anatomy

• Overcame opposition to his methods and findings

**e** The source is useful because it:

• shows that Geminus borrowed Vesalius' illustrations from *The Fabric of the Human Body*

• was published two years after Vesalius's 'Fabric' in England

• shows they had the same illustrations with the background removed; the quality of the illustrations shows Renaissance artwork for its realism and detail

• must have been popular for three editions to have been published.

## Page 25

**a** A soothing cream after surgery; 'crow's beak clamp'; use of ligatures; better false limbs

**b** Clowes quoted Paré; acknowledged his work; used some of his ideas in his books; popularised him

**c** Galen believed that blood was the body's fuel.

**d** Harvey calculated, observed, experimented and investigated for himself. He read widely to find out what other scientists had said before him.

**e** Features of the Renaissance you might mention:

**Printing**:

• medical pioneers all produced important books e.g. Vesalius (1543), Paré (1575), Harvey (1628)

• explain the importance to printing, but point to other factors as follows

**Overcoming opposition**:

• centuries of ancient Hippocratic and Galenic knowledge difficult to overturn for the Renaissance scientists

• Catholic Church supported the ancient knowledge which meant critics could be seen as heretics

• scientists needed a powerful patron e.g. Vesalius and Holy Roman Emperor Charles V, or had to wait a long time to be recognised e.g. Harvey

**Critical scientific approach**:

• in the Renaissance scientists and doctors discovered new accurate knowledge

• proved their conclusions e.g. Vesalius showed how Galen was wrong; Paré'spatients recovered more quickly without pain; Harvey's predictions proved right when powerful microscope invented to show the link between arteries and veins

**Conclusion**:

• printing spread new information but it was the courage and the science of the medical pioneers of the Renaissance that was the main characteristic

## Chapter 5
## Page 27

**a** **New treatments**: new natural medicines such as Cinchona bark for malaria, opium for pain, lemons and limes to treat scurvy

**Traditional treatments**: bloodletting, royal touch to cure scrofula

**b** You should produce your own spider diagram for this activity.

**c** In both the seventeenth century and the Middle Ages there were traditional treatments using herbs, bloodletting and purging, and astrology. Supernaturally based treatments still existed in the forms of spells, and a belief in the power of the royal touch to cure scrofula. Treatments for and explanations of the plague in 1348 and the seventeenth century were similar in that victims were bled in both times and there was a belief in poisoned air.

Some new treatments in the seventeenth century were quinine for malaria, opium for pain, and lemon and limes to treat scurvy. But the seventeenth century and the Middle Ages were similar in that there were new treatments, often from the Islamic world, such as new drugs e.g. senna andnaphtha, and also criticism of Galen e.g. about the circulation of the blood. Treatment of the plague in 1665 often involved identification and quarantine which was new and showed some small success.

## Page 29

**a** Wealthy businessmen or private subscriptions from individuals

**b** • They were available to hundreds of patients, not just usually 12 as had been the case in the Middle Ages.

• The aim of a Medieval hospital was to care for the sick whereas eighteenth-century hospitals tried to cure their patients.

• Some Medieval hospitals had no doctors but were staffed by priests and nuns, whereas eighteenth-century hospitals not only had doctors but tried to train them.

• Medieval hospitals were based on the idea that illness might be a punishment for sin or was certainly God's will whereas eighteenth-century hospitals adopted a more evidence-based scientific approach to illness.

**c** Hunter challenged the accepted view that he should amputate the leg of a man with an aneurysm; he saved the leg by encouraging new blood vessels to grow.

**d** **Warfare**: had been an army surgeon

**Individual ability**: was even prepared to experiment on himself regarding venereal disease

**Scientific method**: experimented with narrow blood vessels, he did experiments on himself, observed anatomical specimens

**Communication**: wrote several books e.g. *The Natural History of the Teeth*

**e** This painting is useful because it has in it some of the anatomical specimens that Hunter collected. It shows that he published books about what he observed. His reputation grew because he trained many other surgeons e.g. Edward Jenner. This painting was done after Hunter died therefore people must have recognised his achievements and thought they and he were worth commemorating in the picture.

## Chapter 6
### Page 31

SIGNIFICANCE

**a** Jenner gave an eight-year-old boy cowpox. After the illness had passed, he gave the boy smallpox. The boy did not die because cowpox had protected him.

**b** Smallpox could kill, cause blindness,and leave people very disfigured. Inoculation could help but if it was done inexpertly this also could kill.

**c** Inoculation

**Definition**: Gives you a weaker form of disease so that you develop immunity to the stronger form

**When popular**: Eighteenth century

**Problems/drawbacks**: Inoculated people could pass on smallpox; cost money so poor could not afford it;limited understanding about how it worked; religious objections

**Celebrity/royal endorsement**: Lady Mary Wortley Montagu

**Vaccination**

**Definition**: Gives you a different non-lethal disease that provides you with immunity against a similar but lethal disease

**When popular**: After 1798

**Problems/drawbacks**: People did not understand how it worked; attempts to copy it could fail through contamination; snobbery around Jenner not being a fashionable city doctor

**Celebrity/royal endorsement**: British royal family, British government

**d** Answers might include reference to:
- saving lives
- adopting a scientific approach
- finding a safer method of protecting against smallpox than inoculation
- gaining the recognition/involvement of the government in preventing disease
- showing the value of celebrity endorsement of a new treatment.

## Chapter 7
### Page 33

SIMILARITY

**a** Pain could not be controlled or removed. Pain-relieving substances were difficult to judge and could be deadly. Therefore surgeons operated quickly to reduce the amount of pain felt by the patient.

**b** 1842 – Crawford Long (removed a neck growth using ether)

1844 – Horace Wells (used nitrous oxide to remove teeth)

1846 – Robert Liston (amputated a leg using ether)

1847 – James Simpson (discovered chloroform)

1848 – Hannah Greener (died under anaesthetic)

1853 – Queen Victoria (used chloroform as an anaesthetic during childbirth)

**c and d** Answers might include the following similarities:
- Opposition within the medical profession – doctors were used to operating quickly and making money from using inoculation
- There were accidents/deaths at first – Hannah Greener for example
- Both problems– smallpox and pain – were feared
- There was official approval that encouraged take up and overcame opposition – Queen Victoria and the British government

### Page 35

SIMILARITY

**a** They could see microbes through a microscope.
- They did not know germs caused disease.
- They thought germs appeared after infection.
- They thought all germs were pretty much the same.

**b** They thought the germs generated spontaneously in wounds, caused by a chemical reaction, because the person was weak.

**c** You should produce your own set of revision cards for this activity.

**d** Both were good scientists – but the opposition to both men's theories was similar because they did not have conclusive proof despite the fact that they tested their theories by experiment, recorded results, and published these results: Harvey in 1628, Lister in 1867.

There was strong opposition to both because they questioned established belief – Harvey criticised Galen, Lister criticised spontaneous generation.

### Page 37

FACTORS

**a** Cattle plague showed that specific microbes were responsible, the disease was spread by contact, and quarantine worked. It showed the value of science and technology – by using microscopes.

**b** Koch identified typhoid germs and showed that anti-contagionists were wrong because typhoid did not occur spontaneously where there was dirt.

**c** Aseptic surgery tries to exclude germs from the area of an operation.

**d** Lister's work was very important.

The cattle plague showed a specific microbe could cause epidemics.

Tyndall helped to publicise Lister's work and Pasteur's Germ Theory. He took on Charlton Bastian and spontaneous generation. He was helped in the 1870s by British scientists and doctors.

## Chapter 8
### Page 39

SOURCE ANALYSIS

**a** Factors include war (France and Germany were rivals); government and finance (governments paid for Pasteur's and Koch's laboratories and teams); character (both men were very determined scientists); luck (accidentally weakened chicken cholera germs led to a vaccine); teamwork (teams helped Pasteur with rabies, and to identify germs); competition (both scientists wanted to make discoveries before the other did); communication (both men published news of their discoveries, news spread quickly by telegraph)

**b** Fact file could include: German doctor; identified specific germs e.g. anthrax (1876), cholera (1884) and TB (1882); started science of bacteriology; devised tools to hunt bacteria e.g. agar jelly and staining; devised method of concentrating and isolating specific germs

**c** The cartoon is very useful because: it is from an English newspaper and – even though Koch is German – it acknowledges his achievement, which shows his fame had spread; it recognises his achievement by comparing him to a national saint – St George; it shows people understood how he made his discoveries – by identifying his tools (the microscope); it shows how important Koch's work was in defeating the big killer disease – TB – which is shown as a snake; symbolically it shows how Koch's microscope sheds light upon the dark origins of TB.

## Chapter 9
### Page 41

SOURCE ANALYSIS

**a** Answers might include:
- people moved from the countryside to cities like London, Sheffield, Birmingham, Leeds and Manchester to work in the new factories that were built during the Industrial Revolution
- the factories needed thousands of workers to operate the machinery that made cloth, pottery, iron or steel.

**b** You should produce your own set of revision cards for this activity.

**c** Answers might include:
- it helps to show overcrowding – and overcrowding was linked to the easier spread of contagious diseases such as tuberculosis
- it shows outside toilets, shared by many, next to many houses which helps to explain the spread of diseases linked to contamination like cholera and typhoid
- as it is from a government inquiry, it shows that people at the time thought epidemics were a problem, and they were concerned about why disease spread in the cities.

## Page 43

a **back-to-back housing**: a form of terraced housing, built close together in rows

**miasma theory**: a belief that disease was spread by an 'infectious mist' given off by rotting animals, rubbish and human waste

**cholera**: a painful and deadly disease common in the nineteenth century, with no known cure at that time

**laissez-faire**: the idea that the government should not interfere in the lives of ordinary people and force them to change

**Great Stink**: a time in the summer of 1858 when the stench from the River Thames was so strong that politicians in the Houses of Parliament (right next to the river) demanded to meet somewhere else

b You should produce your own spider diagram for this activity.

c You should list information for the following dates – 1837, 1838, 1842, 1848, 1853, 1854, 1858, 1866, 1867, 1874, 1875

d The politician is throwing out laws to the pigs, who are the councillors. Under his arm he has sanitary measures and on the law papers are written, 'improved sewage', 'cleanliness' and 'Health of Towns Bill'. The councillors or pigs are ignoring them.

e You might write that it helps us to understand the development of public health at this time because it shows councillors who are not interested in public health laws. Perhaps they have a laissez-faire attitude. They are shown as pigs who snuffle around in filth. *Punch* magazine is showing what many people thought of those who resisted public health improvements, by poking fun at them for their ignorance and self-interest. The cartoon shows an attitude to people who resisted improvements in public health in the mid-nineteenth century. It suggests that not reforming public health is inhuman, and that only animals like filth.

## Chapter 10
## Page 45

a **magic bullet**: a chemical that finds and kills specific bacteria in the body

**Staphylococcus**: a highly resistant bacteria which can cause food and blood poisoning

**antibiotic**: a medicine (such as penicillin) that can destroy or weaken certain microbes

b **Paul Ehrlich** was Koch's assistant. He worked at finding a chemical that would not only stain a specific type of bacteria, but kill it too. He discovered a chemical cure for syphilis in 1909. After this, other 'magic bullets' were found by scientists over the next 20 years.

**Alexander Fleming** was a bacteriologist working at St Mary's Hospital, London. By chance, in 1928 he left several plates of germs on a bench before going on holiday. When he came back, he noticed a large blob of mould in one of the dishes. Staphylococcus germs next to the mould had been killed. He discovered it was penicillin. He realised the germ-killing capabilities of penicillin and published his findings that year. He did not inject penicillin into an infected animal. This would have shown that penicillin could be used as a medicine, and could kill infections in the body without harming living cells. Few people regarded Fleming's work as a major breakthrough and gradually even Fleming himself lost interest in it.

c Pasteur used weakened forms of the bacteria to allow the body to build up immunity to the disease if it struck again. Ehrlich found a chemical that would not only stain a specific type of bacteria but kill it too.

d **Role of the individual**: Fleming's commitment to his work

**Science and technology**: Fleming was a bacteriologist, worked in a science lab, and worked scientifically once the discovery had been made; he published his findings in a science journal

**Chance**: after leaving dishes of germs on a bench unattended while on holiday, Fleming returned to find that mould had developed in one of the dishes and that the germs next to it were dead

**War**: Fleming was sent by St Mary's Hospital in London to study the treatment of wounded soldiers in the First World War; after the war, Fleming became determined to find a better way to treat infected wounds and conducted detailed experiments

**Communication**: published his findings so others could read them

## Page 47

a Part of a research team from Oxford University:

- applied to the British government for some money to begin further research into the germ-killing powers of penicillin
- received only £25 but pressed on and successfully tested penicillin on mice, then a human
- in June 1941, Florey met with the US government who agreed to pay several huge chemical companies to make millions of gallons of penicillin

b You could add Florey and Chain to 'role of the individual' and the need for penicillin to treat wounded soldiers in the Second World War to 'war'.

c You may not be able to add a note for 'religion', but could note for 'government' the fact that Florey met with the US government, who agreed to pay several huge chemical companies to make millions of gallons of penicillin.

d **War**: the USA entered the Second World War in 1941. War created a powerful motive for the US government to provide funds to develop penicillin. Penicillin was important to help wounded soldiers recover and fight infection. War prevented British drug companies from trying to develop penicillin because they were preoccupied with producing existing medicines and had no extra capacity for research.

**Role of the individual**: Fleming had the insight to realise that something from the mould had killed the germs. He assumed incorrectly that penicillin would not work in a glass test tube full of contaminated blood. Florey tested penicillin in living tissue and found that it did work – it killed bacteria. Florey had the insight and courage to pursue the development of penicillin, a decision that might have brought disapproval if penicillin had failed.

**Government**: the US government put their authority and resources behind penicillin which convinced the drug companies to commit to it. The government forced US drug companies to exchange information about the mass production of penicillin.

**Conclusion**: at different points in the development of penicillin different factors had a crucial influence. The role of the individual was important in the development from 1938 but on his own Florey would not have been able to mass-produce penicillin or confirm how effective it was. That depended on the resources of business and government working together to help win the war.

## Page 49

a **antibiotic resistance**: the ability of bacteria to resist the effects of an antibiotic to which they were once sensitive

**alternative therapies**: ways of treating illness that do not rely on mainstream, doctor-dispensed scientific medicine

b You should produce your own set of examples for this activity.

c You might write that there are a number of reasons, which can be broken down into categories. For example, **new technology**, such as keyhole surgery and MRI scanning, has helped doctors and surgeons to develop new techniques for identifying illnesses and operating on them. Also, the **communication** of new treatments and ideas has spread rapidly due to the increased use of television, news media and the Internet. Television and radio **campaigns** have made more people than ever before aware of health risks associated with smoking and alcohol, for example

d You might refer to the following significance:

- as medical science defeats diseases so new medical problems emerge as a threat
- antibiotic resistance can be caused by the overuse of antibiotics
- new antibiotics are very expensive to research and develop.

## Chapter 11
### Page 51
**FACTORS**

**a** You might write that governments spend lots of money on the development of the latest medical techniques and the most up-to-date medical technology to get more soldiers fitter quicker and back on the battlefield. Also, doctors and surgeons work very hard in wartime, often in battlefield situations, to develop their ideas in order to treat the injured. Also, the huge numbers of wounded soldiers give doctors and surgeons more opportunities than are available in peacetime to test their ideas out.

**b** **Marie Curie**: developed mobile X-ray units for use near the battlefield in the First World War

**Harold Gillies**: London-based army doctor who set up a special unit to graft (transplant) skin and treat men suffering from severe facial wounds in the Second World War

**Archibald McIndoe**: in the Second World War, used new drugs such as penicillin to prevent infection when treating pilots with horrific facial injuries; his work on reconstructing damaged faces and hands was respected all over the world

**Albert Hustin**: discovered that glucose and sodium citrate stopped blood from clotting on contact with air

**c** **Public health:**
- diet – food shortages during wartime meant people grew their own food; this improved people's diets because the food they grew – fresh vegetables for example – was very healthy
- hygiene and disease – in order to keep Britain 'fighting fit' during the Second World War, there was a campaign that warned against the dangers of poor hygiene; a national immunisation programme against diphtheria was launched, for example
- other scientific and medical developments during wartime also eventually benefited the general public (for example, X-rays and blood transfusions)

**In the fight against infection:**
- drugs to counter infection developed during the Second World War (for example penicillin, the first antibiotic); the British and US governments realised how important this new 'wonder drug' could be in curing infections in deep wounds; by 1944, enough penicillin was produced to treat all the Allied forces in Europe

### Page 53
**SOURCE ANALYSIS**

**a** You will compile your own definitions, but you may write something like this, for example:
**keyhole surgery**: operations performed through small cuts using miniaturised

instruments and small fibre-optic cameras linked to computers; **laser surgery**: surgery using lasers (rather than a scalpel); **radiation therapy**: the use of high-energy radiation to shrink tumours and kill cancer cells

**b** Examples might include:

**war**: urgent increase in production of penicillin by the Allies in the Second World War

**superstition and religion**: distrust of traditional remedies led people to explore alternative treatments, sometimes with positive results

**chance**: Fleming's work on penicillin

**government**: free vaccines have been available in the UK for many diseases
**communication**: national media campaigns such as the school 'Healthy Eating Standards'

**science and technology**: use of latest technology in laser surgery and keyhole surgery

**the role of the individual in encouraging or inhibiting change**: many individuals to choose from

**c** The source is useful because it shows that:
- the government knew that in wartime their medical services would be under pressure
- the government needed to react to the dangers they thought war would bring
- some types of medicine can develop at a greater rate during wartime than in peacetime – in this case the development of blood transfusion units (the British National Blood Transfusion Service opened in 1938); large blood banks were developed in both the USA and Britain during the Second World War
- during wartime, governments spend lots of money on the development of the latest medical techniques; they know that if medical services are good, then more injured soldiers will get fitter quicker and back on the battlefield.

## Chapter 12
### Page 55
**SOURCE ANALYSIS**

**a** Answers might include:
- the government was worried that Britain couldn't defend itself with a weak army
- Germany, a rival nation, had a system of welfare, and was beginning to produce as much coal, iron and steel as Britain; some politicians believed that the government should get directly involved in public health and welfare to boost the productivity of the nation
- the Booth and Rowntree reports had an impact too – and the Liberal Party was also worried about the popularity of the Labour Party, which had been founded in 1900, so they wanted measures that would appeal to working people and stop them voting for Labour.

**b** You should produce your own set of revision cards for this activity.

**c** The source is useful because it shows that:
- the government was interested in their reforms
- the free school meals made an immediate impact on children's weights – and these weights dropped when the children were not at school
- children were gaining weight, but this increased rapidly when the free school meals were introduced in mid-April 1907.

### Page 57
**SIMILARITY**

**a** Answers might include: Liberal reforms after 1906; building of back-to-back housing banned; local councils had to provide health visitors, clinics for pregnant women, and day nurseries (1918); councils began to build new houses for poorer families (1919); slum clearance programme (1930s); formation of the NHS; twelve new towns were created; 280,000 council homes were being built each year (by 1948)

**b** **Charles Booth**: investigated the poor in London and published *Life and Labour of the People in London*

**Seebohm Rowntree**: investigated the poor in York and published *Poverty: A Study of Town Life*

**Sir William Beveridge**: social reformer and economist, published the Beveridge Report

**Clement Atlee**: leader of the Labour government who introduced the NHS and many suggestions from the Beveridge Report

**Aneurin Bevan**: Labour Minister for Health who help form the NHS in 1948

**c** You should produce your own spider diagram for this activity.

**d** **Reasons why public health improved in the nineteenth century:**
- developments such as sewers
- discoveries by Pasteur (Germ Theory), Snow (cause of cholera) etc.
- work of Chadwick to raise awareness
- action by governments (end of laissez-faire) with public health acts, for example.

**Reasons why public health improved in the twentieth century:**
- action by governments (e.g. Liberal Reforms), NHS, education
- impact of war
- discoveries of Fleming etc.

**Make comparisons** – individuals, government action, science and technology

**anaesthetic**  substance that removes pain

**anatomy**  science of understanding the structure and internal organs of the body

**antibiotic**  medications used to cure, and in some cases prevent, bacterial infections; they are not effective against viruses such as the common cold

**aseptic**  state of being completely free of harmful microbes; sterilising to create a contamination-free environment

**barber-surgeon**  Medieval barber who practiced surgery and dentistry

**bloodletting**  Medieval medical treatment of removing some blood from a patient by opening a vein or using leeches to suck it out

**bubonic plague**  plague spread by the bite of a flea; buboes are lumps

**cauterisation**  using a heated iron to stop bleeding and seal a wound

**cesspit**  pit for the disposal of liquid waste and sewage

**epidemic**  spread of a disease to a large number of people

**humours**  the theory of the four humours is based on the idea that everything was made of the four elements of fire, wind, earth and water; and that elements exist as different liquids in the body

**inoculation**  using weakened but live germs of a disease in a healthy person to build up an immunity (resistance) against the stronger form of the same disease

**lay people**  ordinary people who were not monks or priests

**miasma**  name given to what people thought was an 'infectious mist' given off by rotting animals, rubbish and human waste; many believed it caused illness and disease

**microbe**  living organism that is too tiny to be seen without a microscope; includes bacteria, which can cause diseases

**pilgrimage**  journey, of devotion or of moral significance, to visit a holy place

**pneumonic plague**  plague spread by breathing in germs from the infected lungs of a bubonic plague victim

**public health**  health of the population as a whole

**quarantine**  confining or stopping people from going in or out of a place

**spontaneous generation**  theory that microbes appear as if by magic, and that germs are the result of disease

**spore**  cell or small organism that can grow into a new organism in the correct conditions

**trepanning**  drilling holes in the head

**vaccination**  using the dead germs of a disease or one similar to it to build up an immunity (resistance) against the stronger form of the disease

**Notes**

**Notes**

**Notes**

# Topics available from *Oxford AQA GCSE History*

## Student Books and Kerboodle Books

**Paper One: understanding the modern world**

**Period Study**

**Germany 1890–1945 Democracy and Dictatorship**
Student Book
978 019 837010 9
Kerboodle Book
978 019 837014 7

**America 1920–1973 Opportunity and Inequality**
Student Book
978 019 841262 5
Kerboodle Book
978 019 841263 2

**Wider World Depth Study**

**Conflict and Tension: The Inter-War Years 1918–1939**
Student Book
978 0 19 837011 6
Kerboodle Book
978 019 837015 4

**Conflict and Tension between East and West 1945–1972**
Student Book
978 019 841266 3
Kerboodle Book
978 019 841267 0

**Conflict and Tension in Asia 1950–1975**
Student Book
978 019 841264 9
Kerboodle Book
978 019 841265 6

**Conflict and Tension: First World War 1894–1918**
Student Book
978 019 842900 5
Kerboodle Book
978 019 842901 2

**Paper Two: Shaping the nation**

**Thematic Study**

**Thematic Studies c790–Present Day**
Student Book
978 019 837013 0
Kerboodle Book
978 019 837017 8

Contents include **all 3 Thematic Study options:** Health, Power, and Migration, Empires and the People

**British Depth Study**

**British Depth Studies c1066–1685**
Student Book
978 019 837012 3
Kerboodle Book
978 019 837016 1

Contents include **all 4 British Depth Study options:** Norman, Medieval, Elizabethan, and Restoration England

---

## Covering all 16 options

### Teacher Handbook

**Teacher Handbook**
978 019 837018 5

### Kerboodle Exam Practice and Revision

**Kerboodle Exam Practice and Revision**
978 019 837019 2

## Revision Guides  📖 RECAP  ⚙ APPLY  🔄 REVIEW  ✓ SUCCEED

**Germany 1890–1945 Democracy and Dictatorship**
Revision Guide: 978 019 842289 1
Kindle edition: 978 019 842290 7

**America 1920–1973 Opportunity and Inequality**
Revision Guide: 978 019 843282 1
Kindle edition: 978 019 843283 8

**Conflict and Tension: The Inter-War Years 1918–1939**
Revision Guide: 978 019 842291 4
Kindle edition: 978 019 842292 1

**Conflict and Tension between East and West 1945–1972**
Revision Guide: 978 019 843288 3
Kindle edition: 978 019 843289 0

**Conflict and Tension in Asia 1950–1975**
Revision Guide: 978 019 843286 9
Kindle edition: 978 019 843287 6

**Britain: Power and the People c1170–Present Day**
Revision Guide: 978 019 843290 6
Kindle edition: 978 019 843291 3

**Health and the People c1000–Present Day**
Revision Guide: 978 019 842295 2
Kindle edition: 978 019 842296 9

**Norman England c1066–c1100**
Revision Guide: 978 019 843284 5
Kindle edition: 978 019 843285 2

**Elizabethan England c1568–1603**
Revision Guide: 978 019 842293 8
Kindle edition: 978 019 842294 5

---

Order online at **www.oxfordsecondary.co.uk/aqa-gcse-history**

## OXFORD